CONVERSATIONAL HYPNOSIS AND NLP

PUBLISHED BY WWW,BIGFONTBOOKS.COM

ISBN-13: **978-1-940849-66-9**
ISBN-10: 1-940849-66-7

Contents

The Presuppositions of NLP   5
Anchoring   7
 'Anchoring' and Learning   8
Conversational Hypnosis 11
 METABOLISM CHANGE   12
 HINDSIGHT   13
 WHEEL CHAIR   13
 CITY- STATE- COUNTRY   14
 MATURE LOOKING 14
 SET (SUGARS) 15
 BEWARE - 3   16
 SCALE OF DESIRE   16
 VERBAL TALK 17
 ICE SCULPTURE   18
 3 WAYS TO RESPOND   19
 GOD   20
 VIDEO OF EATING   20
 HOT STOVE   21
 HAND TO FACE   21
 DELIVER SUGGESTIONS,
 AS THE CLIENT RESPONDS.   22
 THE POWER   22
 RADIO WAVES   23
 SIX SHOOTER 23
 CHANGING CHAIRS   24
 RAPID TALK   25
 CANDY IN THE MUD   26
 A NEW YOU   26
 TIME DISTORTION 27
 SODA BOTTLE FOR WATER   28
 ALARM CLOCK   28
 A BUDGET   29
 GOOD LEARNING EXPERIENCE 30
 ANTICIPATION   30
 BIG LOTTERY 31
 DEEP SNOW   32
 DOG WITH A BONE 32
 PERCENT OF LOSS   33

 NO WILL POWER   33
 ELEPHANT   34
 HEAR - SEE - FEEL - KNOW   35
 GRANDPARENTS   35
 FRIENDS   36
 RED   36
 LICENSE PLATES   37
 THE ROAD RUNNER   37
 EAT A FLOWER   38
 MONEY WASTED   38
 STATE LOCATION   41
 RETIREMENT TIME 41
 TIME SMOKING   42
 DEFECT 42
 NOT LOGICAL   43
 LOOKS LIKE YOU NEEDED   43
 NASTY   44
 SPECIAL CHAIR   44
 ALL YOU CAN EAT   44
 HAMMER   45
 BINGES   45
 60 SECONDS   46
 TODAY'S DATE   46
 WORD OF HONOR (IDEO)   47
 WORD OF HONOR (MENTAL)   47
 ADULTS ARE CHILDREN
 GROWN TALL 48
 10 STOP SIGNS   48
 SENSITIVE ARM   49
 CHANGING SIDES   50
 THE MUSIC IS GONE   50
 BOWLING   51
 WORKING OUT   51
 THE FUTURE   52
 THINKING   52
 SHOE TAP   53
 JUNK FOOD   53
 CHILD INDUCTION # 1   54
 FEAR - NOT EXITING   54
 FEAR TELLING   55
 FEAR - CONTROL   55

HYPNOTIZED YES NO   56
MIND WANDERING 56
ALMOST ASLEEP   56
THE WATCH   57
NOT COMPARED TO   57
ANYONE WITH NORMAL 58
3 MINUTE RULE   58
THE BOOKS   59
KITCHEN TABLE   60
INVESTMENT 61
REJECT   61
SMALL CLOTHING   62
DIABETIC   63
TYPEWRITER 63
ONLY ONE COOKIE 64
ORDER AT A RESTAURANT   65
LIPSTICK   65
THE PRESIDENT   66
3 GODS   66
DRUGS 67
100% EFFORT (SMOKING) 67
3 CATEGORIES (SMOKING)   68
FOURTH CATEGORY   68
WHAT IF?   69
A $ 5.00 CAR   69
HEALTH CLUB PAYMENT 70
TIME DISTORTION (TEST)   70
SAYING THE ALPHABET   71
TIME WASTED   72
RELAXED ATTITUDE   72
BECOME THE BEST DRIVER   73
ASPIRIN   73
THROW AWAY FOOD   74
LARGE PACK   74
SHOT GLASS   75
THE BEACH   76
MEMORY 2   77
TAKE A BREAK   77
TRAY OF GLASSES   78
FASTING   79
DRIVE THRU 80
ICE BOX   81
SUPERIOR   81

FIRST DATE   82
REFRAMING 83
REFRAMING (CONSCIOUS)   83
FAN INDUCTION   84
THUMB & FINGER   85
SPORTS CAR   85
ACTOR 86
TEN STORES   87
THE COFFEE TASTER   87
MAGIC BUTTON   88
GIFT AS A CHILD   88
CHANGING THE EVENT 89
MEMORY   90
LEARNING THE ALPHABET   91
NEED TO, HAVE TO 92
100% EFFORT (WEIGHT) 92
PROBLEMS WITH SCALE'S   92
EVIL HYPNOTIST   93
1/2 A GALLON OF ICE CREAM   93
3 CATEGORIES (WEIGHT) 94
CAKE   94
HOUSE FIRE 95
CREATE DESIRE FOR   95
COMMAND   96
CHANGING THE GOAL   97
I DON'T THINK I CAN   97
HAND SHAKE 98
GOOD FEELING FOR SAYING NO 99
ASKING 4 TIMES   100
YOUR FUTURE   100
A MANURE FIELD 101
NLP and Spirituality   103
    Studying the sedative 103

The Presuppositions of NLP

The thirteen presuppositions are the central principles central of NLP; they are its guiding philosophy, its 'beliefs'. These principles are not claimed to be true or universal. You do not have to believe they are true. They are called presuppositions because you pre-suppose them to be true and then act as if they were. You then discover what happens. If you like the results then continue to act as if they are true. They form a set of ethical principles for life.

1. People respond to their experience, not to reality itself.

We do not know what reality is. Our senses, beliefs, and past experience give us a map of the world from which to operate. A map can never be exactly accurate; otherwise it would be the same as the ground it covers. We do not know the territory, so for us, the map is the territory. Some maps are better than others for finding your way around. We navigate life like a ship through a dangerous area of sea; as long as the map shows the main hazards, we will be fine. When maps are faulty and do not show the dangers, then we are in danger of running aground. NLP is the art of changing these maps, so we have greater freedom of action.

2. Having a choice is better than not having a choice.

Always try to have a map for yourself that gives you the widest and richest number of choices. Act always to increase choice. The more choices you have, the freer you are and the more influence you have.

3. People make the best choice they can at the time.

A person always makes the best choice they can, given their map of the world. The choice may be self-defeating, bizarre or evil, but for them, it seems the best way forward. Give them a better choice in their map of the world and they will take it. Even better give them a superior map with more choices in it.

4. People work perfectly.

No one is wrong or broken. They are carrying out their strategies perfectly, but the strategies may be poorly designed and ineffective. Find out how you and others do what they do so their strategy can be changed to something more useful and desirable.

5. All actions have a purpose.

Our actions are not random; we are always trying to achieve something, although we may not be aware of what that is.

6. Every behaviour has a positive intention.

All our actions have at least one purpose - to achieve something that we value and benefits us. NLP separates the intention or purpose behind an action from the action itself. A person is not their behaviour. When a person has a better choice of behaviour that also achieves their positive intention, they will take it.

7. The unconscious mind balances the conscious; it is not malicious.

The unconscious is everything that is not in consciousness at the present moment. It contains all the resources we need to live in balance.

8. The meaning of the communication is not simply what you intend, but also the response you get.

This response may be different to the one you wanted. There are no failures in communication, only responses and feedback. If you are not getting the result you want, change what you are doing. Take responsibility for the communication.

9. We already have all the resources we need, or we can create them.

There are no unresourceful people, only unresourceful states of mind.

10. Mind and body form a system. They are different expressions of the one person.

Mind and body interact and mutually influence each other. It is not possible to make a change in one without the other being affected. When we think differently, our bodies change. When we act differently we change our thoughts and feelings.

11. We process all information through our senses.

Developing your sense so they become more acute gives you better information and helps you think more clearly.

12. Modeling successful performance leads to excellence.

If one person can do something it is possible to model it and teach it to others. In this way everyone can learn to get better results in their own way, you do not become a clone of the model – you learn from them

13. If you want to understand - Act. The learning is in the doing.

Anchoring

In NLP, "anchoring" refers to the process of associating an internal response with some environmental or mental trigger, so that the response may be quickly, and sometimes covertly, reaccessed. Anchoring is a process that on the surface is similar to the "conditioning" technique used by Pavlov to create a link between the hearing of a bell and salivation in dogs. By associating the sound of a bell with the act of giving food to his dogs, Pavlov found he could eventually just ring the bell and the dogs would start salivating, even though no food was given. In the behaviorist's stimulus-response conditioning formula, however, the stimulus is always an environmental cue and the response is always a specific behavioral action. The association is considered reflexive and not a matter of choice.

In NLP this type of associative conditioning has been expanded to include links between aspects of experience other than purely environmental cues and behavioral responses. A remembered picture may become an anchor for a particular internal feeling, for instance. A touch on the leg may become an anchor for a visual fantasy or even a belief. A voice tone may become an anchor for a state of excitement or confidence. A person may consciously choose to establish and retrigger these associations for him or herself. Rather than being a mindless knee-jerk reflex, an anchor becomes a tool for self empowerment. Anchoring can be a very useful tool for helping to establish and reactivate the mental processes associated with creativity, learning, concentration and other important resources.

The notion of "anchoring" emerged in NLP when Bandler and Grinder were first modeling the hypnotic techniques of Milton Erickson. Erickson often used or suggested particular cues as posthypnotic triggers to help a person change his or her internal state or reaccess a hypnotic trance. Grinder and Bandler generalized the use of these cues and triggers to include other types of internal processes, without the need of initially establishing a hypnotic state. By 1976 the first NLP anchoring techniques (such as collapsing anchors) were developed.

It is significant that the metaphor of an "anchor" is used in NLP terminology. The anchor of a ship or boat is attached by the members of the ship's crew to some stable point in order to hold the ship in a certain area and keep it from floating away. The implication of this is that the cue which serves as a psychological "anchor" is not so much a mechanical stimulus which "causes" a response as it is a reference point that helps to stabilize a particular internal state. To extend the analogy fully, a ship could be considered the focus of our consciousness on the ocean of experience. Anchors serve as reference points which help us to find a particular location on this experiential sea, and to hold our attention there and keep it from drifting.

Similar to the Metaphor of a Boat or Ship, an Anchor Is a Reference Point that Stabilizes a Particular State The process of establishing an anchor basically involves associating two experiences together in time. In behavioral conditioning models, associations become more strongly established through repetition. Repetition may also be used to strengthen anchors. For example, you could ask someone to vividly re-experience a time she was very creative and pat her shoulder while she is thinking of the experience. If you repeat this once or twice, the pat on the shoulder will begin to become linked to the creative state. Eventually a pat on the shoulder will automatically remind the person of the creative state.

'ANCHORING ' AND LEARNING

A good way to begin to understand the uses of anchoring is to consider how they can be applied in the context of teaching and learning. The process of anchoring, for instance, is an effective means to solidify and transfer learning experiences. In its simplest form, 'anchoring ' involves establishing an association between an external cue or stimulus and an internal experience or state, as in the example of Pavlov ringing the bell for his dogs. A lot of learning relates to conditioning, and conditioning relates to the kind of stimuli that become attached to reactions. An anchor is a stimulus that becomes associated with a learning experience. If you can anchor something in a classroom environment, you can then bring the anchor to the work environment as, minimally, an associative reminder of what was learned.

As an example of this, they did a research study with students in classrooms. They had students learn some kind of task in a certain classroom. Then they split the class in half and put one of the groups in a different room. Then they tested them. The ones who were in the same room where they had learned the material did better on the exams than the students who had been moved to a different room. Presumably this was because there were environmental cues that were associated with the material they had been learning.

We have probably all been in the situation of experiencing something that we wanted to remember, but when we go into a new environment where all the stimuli are so different, it 's easier to forget.

By developing the ability to use certain kinds of anchors, teachers and learners can facilitate the generalization of learning. There will certainly be a greater possibility that learning will be transferred if one can also transfer certain stimuli.

There is another aspect to anchoring related to the fact that Pavlov 's dog had to be in a certain state for the bell to mean anything. The dogs had to be hungry; then Pavlov could anchor the stimulus to the response. Similarly, there is an issue related to what state learners are in, in order to effectively establish an anchor.

For instance, a transparency is a map, but it 's also a stimulus. That is, it gives information, but it can also be a trigger for a reference experience. An effective teacher needs to know when to send a message or not to send a message. If people have a sudden insight — an "Aha! " — and you turn on a transparency, it is going to be received in a different way and associated in a different way than if people are struggling with a concept.

Timing can be very important. It is important for a teacher to time the presentation of material in relation to the state of his or her learners. If the teacher has a cognitive package to present, such as a key word or a visual map, he or she must wait for the moment that the "iron gets hot. " When the teacher senses that there's a kind of a readiness, a surge, or an openness in the group, at that moment he or she would introduce the concepts or show the key words. Because the point of anchoring is that a teacher is not just giving information, he or she is also providing stimuli that gets connected to the reference experiences of the learners. This is why stimuli that are symbolic are often more effective anchors.

The kinds of questions that a teacher needs to answer are, "When do I introduce this idea? " and "How strongly do I want people to experience it, or respond to it? " For example, if the teacher is facilitating a discussion, an issue might arise that is deeply related to beliefs and values that is strongly felt, especially by some people. In that moment, if the presenter puts information out, it becomes connected with that degree of interest or involvement.

The point is that anchoring is not simply a mechanical matter of presenting cognitive maps and giving examples. There 's also the issue of the state of commitment or interest of the learners. Sometimes a teacher will want to let a discussion go on, not just because people are making logical connections, but because the energy level of the group is intensifying, and you want to capture that moment. In other times, if the state of the group is low, the teacher might not want to anchor that state to certain topics or reference experiences.

People may use anchors to re-access resourceful states in themselves as well as in others. It is possible for a teacher, for instance, to use a self-anchor to get into the state he or she desires to be in as a leader of a group. A self-anchor could be an internal image of something that, when thought about, automatically brings on that state; somebody one is close to, for instance. One could also make a self-anchor through an example. Talking about one 's children, or some experience that has a lot of very deep associations.

In summary, anchors employ the process of association to:

• focus awareness
• re-access cognitive knowledge and internal states
• connect experiences together in order to:
- enrich meaning
- consolidate knowledge

• transfer learnings and experiences to other contexts

Cues that are anchors can help to transfer learnings to other contexts. The 'cue' used as an anchor may be either verbal, non-verbal or symbolic (a person may even become an anchor). Common objects and cues from a person's home or working environment may make effective anchors. Some common types of cues used to create anchors include:

Conversational Hypnosis

T = THERAPIST   C = CLIENT

T: How long does it take you to smoke a cigarette?
C: About five Minutes

T: Do you believe that smoking is harmful to your health

C: Yes.

T: Do you ever experience shortness of breath? C: Sometimes.
T: Have you ever burned clothing or other objects?
C: Yes, many times before.
T: Could you find something to do with the money you would be saving? C: Sure I could.
T: Many smokers tell me that it is becoming a headache to smoke, do you agree? C: Oh yes, it's becoming harder to find a place to smoke.
T: Tell me have you ever heard that smoking will decrease your life span?
C: Yes, I have.
T: Wouldn't it be nice to set a positive example for your children?
C: Yes, they hate it when I smoke.
T: As you shared with me earlier you have been smoking about 2 packs a day. Most people who smoke as much as you realize that the majority of their smoking is simply a habit that they really don't think about. The phone rings, and they reach for a cigarette. They start the car and reach for a cigarette.

T: However they do say that there are a few cigarettes that they truly enjoy. Maybe after a meal, or with a cup of coffee.

T: If you were going to be honest with yourself, how many cigarettes do think you really get enjoyment from

C: Maybe four or five.

T: Let's spend a moment and look at your smoking logically rather than emotionally. As you have said yourself, it takes you about 4 or 5 minutes to smoke a cigarette. As you have also told me there may be 4 or 5 that you really do enjoy. That means you are getting about 25 minutes of enjoyment from smoking.

As we both agree it is effecting your health, but what is your health as long as you can have 25 minutes of enjoyment. You burn a few pieces of clothing, furniture, it's becoming a headache to smoke, and you get a little shortness of breath, but what's breathing.

You spend about $700.00 a year, but you make a lot of money. It is a bad example or your children, and it will probably take 5 to 10 years off of your life, but what's living as long as we can have 25 minutes of enjoyment.

T: Don't you agree.
C: Not hardly.

METABOLISM CHANGE

Research has proven that the sub-conscious part of the mind does not have the ability to tell the difference between reality, and imagination.

A few years ago an experiment involving an actor showed how powerful the sub-conscious mind truly is.

In this experiment, the actor's heart rate, breathing, and blood pressure were being monitored. The actor then pretended to be very angry, and upset. Within seconds, his blood pressure began to rise. His heart rate increased. His breathing sped up considerably.

All of his bodily functions began to change simply due to pretending, using his imagination.

The actor was then instructed to pretend that he was slowly walking down a beautiful beach, with not a care in the world. His blood pressure began to drop. His heart rate slowed back down. His breathing became slow, and natural.

So it is easy for us to see that as we imagine something, our sub-conscious will cause the body to respond in exactly the same way as though we were actually involved in the activity.

I want you now to imagine yourself out jogging at a very healthy, and safe pace. Get this image deeply embedded in your mind. Imagine it. Sense it. Feel it now.

As you sit here relaxed, your mind is causing your body t respond as though you were really jogging. Using up the stored excess weight in a very safe, simple, and pleasant manner. You can feel it happening now.

From this moment on, every time you use the telephone your mind will automatically cause your body to respond as though you were actually jogging.

Your mind will continue this process safely until you reach the weight of   pounds. Your mind will then work with you in order to insure your continued success at maintaining your weight at   pounds after you have reduced.

NOTE: YOU MAY USE ANY ACTIVITY THAT THE CLIENT DOES ON A DAILY BASIS INSTEAD OF TALKING ON THE PHONE. SUCH AS DRIVING A CAR, READING A BOOK, ETC.......

HINDSIGHT

Today you will be using a wonderful ability that we call foresight. Thinking ahead.

So often people use hindsight. They wait until it is too late, and then say things like, if I would of known then what I know now. If I only had it to do over again. If I only had another chance.

Today you are using foresight, thinking a head and becoming free of the smoking habit before there could be severe health problems down the road.

By using foresight here, now, today, you are avoiding the possibility of health problems down the road, and finding yourself making statements like. If I would of known then what I know now.

I sure wish I would have quit smoking back in March of 19 _. If I only had it to do over again. I wish I had a second chance.

Well it is not to late for you. You are becoming a non-smoker as of today. It makes you happy to realize that you will not be using hindsight someday in the future.

Discovering that you have the ability to use foresight in any area of your life is always a wonderful, and positive feeling.

WHEEL CHAIR

You are a kind compassionate type of individual. If you would see someone in a wheel chair, you would feel sorry for them but you would also thank God that you have the ability to walk.

If you would see a person that was blind, that had lost their sight, you would feel sorry for them, but would also be relieved that you have ability to see.

If you would encounter, or hear of a person that needs a bottle of oxygen just to walk down the hallway, you would feel sorry for that person, but at the same time you would be so thankful that you had not destroyed your lungs.

So, from this moment on, when you see someone else smoking, you may feel slightly sorry for them, but you, will be pleased, and thankful that you have quit smoking today.

CITY- STATE- COUNTRY

You have decided that the time has come to be free of the smoking habit once and for all.

You are now realizing that there are no cigarettes anywhere in all of St. Louis that could push you back into the smoking habit again.

In fact there are no cigarettes anywhere in Missouri that could control your life, and push you, manipulate you back into smoking.

We can both agree then that there is not a cigarette anywhere in the country that could, or would dominate, control your life again.

From this very moment on there are no longer cigarettes anywhere in the world that could, or would dominate your life again.

You are in control of your own wonderful life.

MATURE LOOKING

T = THERAPIST C = CLIENT

T: I would like you to remember back to one of the first few cigarettes that you ever smoked.

T: As you begin to recall one of those first few cigarettes that you ever smoked, nod your head yes, and relax even further.

WAIT FOR YES RESPONSE T: Tell me about how old were you back then?
C: I was about 15 then.

T: I imagine that one of the reasons that you started smoking back then was to look older or more mature, is that right.

C: Yes, we all wanted to look like sophisticated women back then.

T: Back then at age 15 the cigarettes served a purpose. They did make you look a little older didn't they.

C: We sure thought so.

T: Well the only time that you will ever smoke again is if you really want to look older. Of course today 19 doubt that you want to look older than you are, do you?

C: No.

T: We both can agree then that you will never smoke again unless want to look older.

SET (SUGARS)

You are now SET to loose this excess weight once and for all. You are doing this for your own benefit, and your own personal well being, so this means you can and will achieve total success.

You are truly SET, and ready to win.

SET, S E T. Set, three simple letters. Wouldn't it be wonderful if you could eliminate this excess weight in three simple steps.

I would like you to think about this word SET. S E T.

Think of the S as meaning sugars. Sugars that you no longer need. Think of the E as meaning exercise. Making time for exercising.

Think of the T as meaning table. Always eat only at your table when you

So you are SET. Sugars are a thing of the past. Exercise more. Eating only at the table.

Three simple letters that will lead you to success. S for Sugars being gone. E for exercise. T for the table.

Keep this word, SET in your mind, and enjoy the many, many wonderful changes that you will experience as a direct result of these three powerful letters.

You are now SET to loose this excess weight once and for all.

You are doing this for your own benefit, and your own personal well being, so this means you can and will achieve total success.

You are truly SET, and ready to win.

SET, S E T. Set, three simple letters. Wouldn't it be wonderful if you could eliminate this excess weight in three simple steps.

I would like you to think about this word SET. S E T .

Think of the S as meaning slow. Slow down your eating habits. Think of the E as meaning exercise. Making time for exercising.

Think of the T as meaning table. Always eat only at your table when you are at home. So you are SET. Slow down the eating. Exercise more. Eating only at the table.

Three simple letters that will lead you to success. S for Slow down eating. E for exercise. T for the table.

Keep this word, SET in your mind, and enjoy the many, many wonderful changes that you will experience as a direct result of these three powerful letters.

BEWARE - 3

Now that you are ready to be a nonsmoker once and for all, BEWARE.

Beware, and do not allow any other person, male or female, family member, friend, co-worker, neighbor, or associate, to try and directly or indirectly push you back into the smoking habit.

Beware, and do not allow any situations, circumstances, or set of events, whether they would be calm, tranquil, and pleasant, or nervous, stressful, or rushed, to try and trick you back into this smoking habit again.

Most important of all. BEWARE, and do not allow any thoughts, either your thoughts or some one else's thoughts, from the past, present or ever to arrive in your future, try to trick, or manipulate you back into this silly old smoking habit again.

You will now beware of any, and all possible situations, statements, circumstances, events, thoughts, and individuals that could possibly push you back into smoking.

You will never need to smoke again. You are now in control of your own life, and behaviors.

SCALE OF DESIRE

I would like you to imagine a yardstick with the numbers from 1 to 36 listed on it.
Normally on a yardstick these numbers would represent inches. Today I would like you to think about this yardstick in a totally different way.

If we hold the yardstick in a vertical position we have the number 1 at the bottom, and the number 36 would be at the top, or the highest number.

Let's imagine that each of these numbers now represents your desire to reach a weight of 125 pound.

Think in terms of the number 1 as representing no desire at all to loose this weight, and the number 36 represents the strongest desire for weight loss in the world.

As you now imagine that yard stick, you will begin to notice that one of the numbers is changing. It could be flashing, or spinning. That special number might be growing larger. As soon as you notice one of the numbers changing in any way, I would like you to say that number out loud for me.

C: 24

Good, on a scale of 1 to 36 for desire to reach a weight of 125 pound you are now at a 24.

Spend a moment and now think of yourself at that perfect weight of 125 pounds, and as you do so your desire to loose this weight will increase.

What number is now changing? C: 34

VERBAL TALK

WITH IDEO-MOTOR RESPONSE.

Would the part of the mind that has been keeping Mary over weight now be willing to respond to me verbally? YES RESPONSE.

I want you to tell me why you have been keeping Mary over weight for all these years

C: SHE NEEDS TO STAY OVER WEIGHT. Why does she needs to be over weight?
C: BECAUSE SHE IS A BAD PERSON.

Has she always been a bad person, or was this something that she did recently? C: WHEN SHE WAS 15 YEARS OLD SHE WANTED TO HAVE SEX.
I understand now. You made her gain this weight so that she would no longer be attractive, and that way you would prevent her from engaging in sex at such a young age. Is that right.

C: Yes.

I think that may have been a good decision on your part back at the age of 15. However, Mary is now 31 years old today. Does she really need to be protected any longer?

C: No, I guess not.

You are evidently a very powerful part of Mary's mind. If you wanted to, could you make her get the weight of her body down to a level of 130 pounds?

C: Yes I can do anything to her that I want.
Will you now help her at reaching this level of a 130 pounds, and then protect her by assisting her in maintaining that weight of a 130 pounds.

C: I guess so.

No, guessing is not good enough. I want you to make the same type of commitment that you made when she was 15 years old. You were able to keep her over weight, even when she tried to loose the weight. Now I want you to work with her. Will you make that commitment now?

C: I will get her down to 130 pounds.

Will you work with her to maintain that weight level?

C: She will now be able to reach, and then stay at a weight of a 130 pounds.

How are you going to ensure her success at reaching and maintaining a weight of 130 pounds?

C: I am going to get her to start eating more fruits and vegetables, while at the same time I'll keep her a way from the sweets, and junk foods.

T: I thought you were the most powerful part of her mind, is that all you could think of?

C: You are starting to irritate me. I can do more. I will also get her to exercise more, drink more water, and stop all of the snacking. How is that?

That would be very good, now let's see if you really have the power to do all that you have said.

ICE SCULPTURE

You have done very well in the past at loosing this unwanted weight, but you have reached a plateau that has been holing you back from continuing your progress.

You have told me that it seems as though you were stuck at 155 pounds.

Today we are going to break lose of that plateau of 155 pounds and insure your success at reaching the perfect weight level of 120 pounds.

You will be happy to discover that once you have reached your goal of 120 pounds that will it be a level that you will be stuck at once and for all.

I would like you to imagine an ice sculpture of the numbers of 155. That's right, think of 155 carved in ice. Now think of the sun coming out from behind the clouds, beating down on that ice sculpture.

We both know what is going to happen now.

Your right, the ice is beginning to melt away. That number of 155 is fading, fading away. The thought of 155 pounds is fading away also, and you are ready to continue on with your goal.

As the ice turns to water, it reminds you to drink more water each day to ensure that the plateaus are gone forever.

3 WAYS TO RESPOND

For example sake, during this session if I told you automatically, your right foot was going to float up into the air, it would simply begin to float upwards. Isn't that amazing?

Now, today I am not going to make your foot float up in the air, but if I would tell you, that automatically your right foot would begin to lift up, there would only be three ways in which you could respond.

You could say to yourself, " I really want this to work, so I'll help it out," and then consciously move your foot. I would not want you to do this.

The second way in which you could respond, is to say to yourself, " I won't let it move, and try to keep it from moving". I wouldn't want you to respond in that way either.

The third way, and the way that I would like you to respond is simply, relax, and allow things to take place.

Don't try and make things happen, but don't try and stop them either.

GOD

You have a very strong desire to reach, and maintain a weight of about   pounds.

You are making this commitment for your own good, and your own personal well being. This means that you can, and you will be successful at this goal.

Think about how nice it will be to have the weight of your body to the level of pounds. You will be looking and feeling great in every way.

You have a right to reach, and maintain a weight of   pounds. You have the right to look good.
You have the right to feel good.

In fact you have the right to have a body that is a perfect example of God's own creation of beauty, and health.

This is more than a right, this is an obligation that you are now accepting.

VIDEO OF EATING

Many times an individual who is trying to eliminate negative eating habits tends to think that they must suffer, and me miserable.

In reality, there is nothing miserable about eliminating excess weight, and reaching a level of pounds.

Every person in this country consumes thousands of calories each week, that they really did not care about eating. For example, if I could see a video tape of your eating habits over the last week, I wonder what it would look like.

Now, we do not have such a video, but if we did, and could look at it uninvolved I am sure the following would take place.

If I asked you each time you were eating something the following question. If you did not eat that would you have felt deprived? Your response would most likely be, no.

In fact with most people, there is only about one out of four items that they would say, Yes, I would have really felt deprived or left out if I couldn't of had some of those.

So we all do eat foods; that really were not important to us. Those are the foods that we are now ready to eliminate.

HOT STOVE

As human beginning we sometimes become overly sensitive to what other people are saying to us. For most of us, if we hear another person say, NO we feel rejected, angry, or depressed.

The problem is that we do not spend the time to analyze what that NO really meant. We take it personally, and allow that two-letter word to hurt us.

Imagine a young child about two years old. This young child is in the kitchen with his mother. The mother turns her back for just a moment, and the little boy starts to reach for the hot stove. The mother sees her little boy almost ready to touch the hot stove, and turns around quickly, and

shouts NO.

Well, the little boy is shocked, and his feeling is hurt, he begins to cry. He felt that his mother must not care about him, other wise she would not have told him no.

In reality we understand what the mother was actually saying to the child. Basically the message very much about you, and rather than taking a chance of seeing you injured, I am going to raise the level of my voice, and say no.

HAND TO FACE

NOTE: SHOW CLIENT HOW YOU WOULD LIKE THEM TO HOLD THEIR HAND IN FRONT OF THEIR FACE. PALM OF THE HAND FACING TOWARDS THEM FINGERS PRESSED LIGHTLY TOGETHER. HAND ABOUT EYE LEVEL.

BEGIN WITH PROGRESSIVE RELAXATION AND PROCEED AS FOLLOWS.

In just a moment when, I ask you to, I am going to have you bring one of your hands up in front of your face, fingers extended upwards and pressed together. I am then going to have you try to open your eyes, and pick a spot on your hand. It may seem difficult to open the eyes, and keep them open, which is only natural since you have been relaxing so far. I am going to want you to try, and with a little effort you will at least be able to get them open.

Now, the one thing that you must accomplish is that I want you to remain totally relaxed, and at ease even with your eyes open, and your hand in this position. Remaining relaxed, and at ease, move your hand up in front of your face with fingers pointed upward, and pressed together.

Now, attempt to open your eyes, and pick one spot on your hand, and begin to concentrate on it. As you concentrate on that one spot, and one spot only, your fingers are going to begin to spread apart.

You do not have to make them spread apart, but do not try to stop them. Concentrate and allow things to take place.

Feel them spreading apart NOW. Automatically separating now. It is beginning to feel as though there was a string tied to each finger pulling them apart. Separating further, and wider.

NOTE: ONCE THE FINGERS HAVE SEPARATED, PROCEED IN THE FOLLOWING WAY.

Now, please do not let it disturb you that the drowsy, heavy feeling in your eyes is becoming stronger now that your fingers have spread apart. It is a very normal, natural sensation. As I begin counting from 5 down to 1 that heavy, drowsy feeling will continue to growing stronger.

NOTE: AT THIS POINT BEGIN COUNTING SLOWLY FROM 5 DOWN TO 1 WHILE GIVING SUGGESTIONS FOR EYE CLOSURE.

DELIVER SUGGESTIONS, AS THE CLIENT RESPONDS.
THE POWER

T: I would like you to begin concentrating on the feeling in your right hand. As you concentrate on your right hand you will begin to notice a tingling sensation. As you begin to feel this tingling sensation, I want you to say the word yes, out loud.

C: YES.

T: Good, now notice how that tingling sensation is changing to a pulsating sensation of power, and confidence. As you begin to experience that pulsating sensation of power, and confidence, say the word yes again.

C: YES.

T: Excellent, now notice how that pulsating feeling is now changing into a throbbing sensation of total power. As you feel this throbbing sensation of total power, say the word yes out loud.

C: YES.

T: Now, as you know that you have the power to become free of this smoking habit forever, say the word yes out loud, and take control of your own life. In fact keep saying the word yes, until you know that the smoking habit is gone forever.

C: YES YES YES YES

RADIO WAVES

You may have read, or heard before that we all have great mental abilities that we seldom use. Some people have difficulty in accepting the presence of something that they can not directly see,

At this very moment, there is something in this room, that you can not see, hear or feel, but I assure you it is present.

This room is filled with hundreds of radio waves. That's right in this very room we are actually being bombarded with radio waves.

As you entered the office I am sure that you did not see them. Neither one of us felt these radio waves in the room.
We both could listen very intensely, but we can not hear them. In order to hear the radio waves, we must turn on a radio, and tune it in.

All of us know how to turn on a radio, and how to tune it in to a station in order to hear the radio waves that were around us all the time.

Today you are going to learn to turn on, and tune in to your own subconscious 'abilities. Just like the unused radio waves, you have many abilities that have been with you all along, but they were not utilized before today.

SIX SHOOTER

I would like you to imagine the following situation with me. Think about a man that was told by his doctor, that if he ever smoked a cigarette again, he definitely would die instantly.

This man leaves the doctor's office, and is confused about what he had just heard. He wonders to himself, is that really true, would I die instantly if I smoked a single cigarette?

The man decides to get a few more opinions. He travels to a second, third, fourth, fifth, and a sixth doctor. After an examination the five doctors all told him that they were not sure. They said it is possible that if you smoke another cigarette that you could possibly die instantly.

This man is now driving down the road in his car analyzing what he has been told. One doctor says that I would die instantly, if I ever smoked again, but five other doctors said they were not sure.

As the man drives down the road trying to decide whether or not he should smoke again, he hears a news broadcast on the radio. The newscast is about a man that had just killed himself playing Russian roulette. Apparently the man put a single bullet in a gun that would hold six shells. He then spun the cylinder, put the gun to his head, and pulled the trigger. He died instantly.

The gentleman driving the car was shocked at this newscast.

He wondered how could anyone in their right mind participate in something that deadly.

Even though he had five chances to live, and only one to die, it seems like such a waste to gamble one's life away.

Instantly the man driving the car realized how closely this situation resembled his own dilemma. One doctor has stated that one cigarette would kill him instantly, while five other doctors were not sure.
The odds were exactly the same. One chance to die, and five chances to possibly live. What should he do.

This man chose to live. He threw his cigarettes out the window and never smoked again.

Now, we both know that this is a made up story, but what would happen if the situations in this story were true?

Would you take that type of gamble with your life? Of course not that is why you are here today, in order to become a nonsmoker forever.

CHANGING CHAIRS

I realize that a few moments ago you walked in this office as a smoker. You have been relaxing while sitting in this chair.
In fact it feels as though that very chair as somehow drained all stress, and tension right out of your body. It feels wonderful to allow that chair to take and keep the stresses of day.

It is now time to allow that chair to take away the smoking habit.

In the same way that you were able to feel the tension leave your body, and flow into that chair, all need for cigarettes will now be leaving your body, and remain in this very chair.

You will know as it begins to happen. Some people will know the smoking habit is leaving by a tingling feeling in the hands. Other people will notice a change in body temperature, or an increased need to swallow.

As you begin to notice any one of these three changes, simply nod your head yes.

It might be the tingling feeling, the change in body temperature, or the need to swallow. As you become aware of any one of these signals, nod your head yes.

That's wonderful. All needs for cigarettes are rapidly leaving your body.

In just a moment, when I ask you to, I am going to have you open your eyes, stand up, and move to the chair to your right.

When I ask you to make this change, you will be leaving all thoughts, and needs for cigarettes in the chair that you are presently sitting in.

Now, you will be able to remain totally relaxed and at ease, even with your eyes open, and even while changing chairs.
When you sit back down in the other chair you will instantly close your eyes, relax, and be free of the smoking habit.

You will notice a pleasant change as you get away from the smoking habit and the chair that now holds your old smoking habit.

Remaining completely relaxed, and at ease, I would like you now to open your eyes, stand up, and go to the other chair.

Sit down, close your eyes, and enjoy the feeling of a nonsmoker.

RAPID TALK

I want you now to begin, and relax the muscles in your feet, and legs. Let this wonderful feeling begin to move up into your calves, and thighs. Let every single muscle, tendon, and ligament in your feet, and legs relax completely.

Day after day those feet, and legs have carried you comfortable, so allow them to relax completely.

Let that relaxed feeling begin to move upwards into your hips, and stomach.

Now that positive relaxed feeling is moving up into your breath in freely, and exhale slowly, chest, and the entire body is beginning to relaxed.

Feel that relaxed feeling, now traveling up into your shoulders. It is feeling as though all tension, and stress was leaving your body.

That relaxed sensation is now traveling up over your neck, and the back of your head. Your forehead is becoming free of tension, stress, and worries.

The muscles in, and around your eyes continue to relax. Your cheeks are relaxing. The right, and left side of your neck is relaxing.

From the top of your head to the bottom of your feet, totally relaxed, and at ease.

CANDY IN THE MUD

I would like you to imagine, a little girl about four years old. Think of this little girl in her own back yard eating a candy bar.

Now imagine that little girl dropping that candy bar, and it falls into the mud. The little girl is sad, disappointed, and she even begins to cry.
To this four-year-old child loosing that candy seems to be one of the worst things that could have ever happened.

Let's now think of that same little girl, but thirty years latter. She is now an intelligent woman. Think of that woman walking down the street, eating a candy bar.
The woman accidentally drops the candy, and it falls to the ground. This time however, she looks down at the candy, and says, "oh well it really wasn't that important". In fact she hardly even gave that candy a second thought.

It is amazing how the same person could encounter the same situation, but respond so dramatically different from one time to the other.

You are now going to begin to respond dramatically different to the thoughts of sugars, and sweets.

In fact you are taking the same attitude as the intelligent woman that had lost her candy. The attitude of "oh well, it really wasn't that important"

A NEW YOU

You are now on your way to reaching, and then maintaining a weight level of   pounds.

Imagine yourself at the weight   of pounds, what a wonderful image, and feeling that is. You deserve to reach this weight level once, and for all.

It is like there is a new you beginning to emerge. A new you in control of your own responses, and actions. A new you looking and feeling better than ever before. Yes, there is a new you taking place, here and now.

Many times people say, " you use that term a lot, a new you. What do you mean by that"?

Well there is a new you starting today. It is like having a second chance. In fact you can actually think of it has starting over, or starting fresh.

When you first came into this world you came in free of all negative thoughts, and habits.

Over the years we have all created many habits. Some of these habits may have been positive, while others were negative.

Today there is a new you starting over. You are keeping the positive habits, and qualities, but are eliminating the negative habits.

So, it is easy to see that there really is a new you beginning to emerge, and take control.

TIME DISTORTION

You have many, many wonderful abilities that you have never totally discovered before. One of the abilities that you have, is an ability that we call "time distortion"

Time distortion is an ability that we have all used at one point in our lives.

There may have been a day when you were having a wonderful time over the weekend, and thought in your mind that it must be around a certain time of day. However, when you looked at your watch, it turned out to be much later than you had anticipated. You had totally lost track of time. This is an example of how time distortion can take place automatically.

Today we are going to use that same ability of time distortion in a specific manner.

When you have gone an hour without smoking, as far as effort it will feel as though it has only been a second.

When you have gone an entire day without smoking, as far will feel as though it has only been a minute.

When you have gone an entire week without smoking, as far as effort it will feel as though it has only been an hour.

So this time you will be totally successful at becoming a nonsmoker. An entire week of being a nonsmoker will seem like the same amount of effort that normally would have been experienced in an hour. A very small amount of effort, for such an important goal.

SODA BOTTLE FOR WATER

We both know how important it is to drink water. I understand that when we consider drinking any form of liquid, that water tends to be at the bottom of the list of possible options.

Many people will think of sodas, when the thought of liquids enters their minds.

One of the reasons, that so many people do not drink more water, is that they simply do not think of-the water until after they have drank soda, or some other form of liquid.

The major soda companies have spent millions of dollars in developing containers that are pleasant to the eye. In doing so, when we open the icebox, and look inside, that great looking large bottle of soda is one of the first things that we see. There may have also been a container of water on the same shelf as the soda, but we never saw it.

Now, I do not want you to leave here, and spend millions of dollars in creating a container for water that will be more noticeable.

Instead, the next time one of those large bottles of soda is empty, I would like you to wash it out, and fill it with water. Then place that new, highly desirably bottle of water back into the icebox.

The next time you open the icebox, you will first see a bottle of soda, but no it is your specially designed water bottle that will be working with you.

ALARM CLOCK

To many times in our lives we tend to blame other events on the way that we are responding.

In reality our own thoughts play an important role in the way that we will be feeling, and the way that we will respond in our daily activities.

This situation may have happened to you at one time or the other.

Think about coming home late at night from a party, or a meeting. You are laying in bed, and notice that it is now 2:00 in the morning, and you need to get up at 6:00 a.m.

You say to yourself, I must get to sleep quickly. Of course the opposite tends to occur. You toss, and turn, and it is now 3:00 in the morning, and you even consider whether it is worth going to sleep for just three hours.

You think in your mind, how awful you will be feeling at work the next day. You think of how you will be dragging, and grumpy. You finally fall asleep. The alarm goes of at 6:00 a.m. You get up, turn off the alarm, and then remember that you only had three hours of sleep, so you put yourself on slump. You go to work moan, and complain about only having three hours of sleep, and you warn everyone to stay away from you, you are grumpy.

Now, the interesting question is. Were you dragging, and grumpy because of the three hours of sleep, or perhaps you were simply following your own suggestions.

What if, the same situation had occurred, but this time you were going on a picnic the next day. This time prior to entering sleep, you said to yourself, well I am only going to have three hours of sleep tonight, but I will have a great time tomorrow, and then tomorrow night I will sleep like a rock.

You would then wake up to the alarm, remember that you only had three hours of sleep, and recall your suggestion from the night before about having a great time today.
The night after the picnic, you would recall your own statements about sleeping like a rock. So you would fall asleep quickly, and sleep soundly.

Most situations, and responses in our lives may be traced back to a suggestion that we have given ourselves.

So, I would like you to only implant positive thoughts, and suggestions that will help you in

A BUDGET

The time has come for you to start taking care of yourself.

It appears that you first take care of the children, your husband, your friends, neighbors, co- workers, and strangers. Then if there is any time left over, then you take care of yourself.

Guess what? There will never be any time left over if you put yourself on the bottom of the list.

I have always associated, taking care of yourself with a young couple trying to save money. If they say to themselves, we will pay all of our bills, and then what ever is left over at the end of the month goes into the savings account. For most people there will never be anything left over.

If the young couple started each month by taking blank dollars and putting it in the bank, they would still pay all of the bills.

It works exactly the same way with you. If you would first take time out for yourself, you would still do all of the things for the people who are important in your life.

So from this moment on, let's do things in the opposite way. Start taking time for you FIRST, and then see how great you feel about being there for the other people in your life.

GOOD LEARNING EXPERIENCE

T = THERAPIST C = CLIENT

T: Did one of those cigarettes sneak up and get you? C: Yes, I'm afraid so.
T: Tell me, what was happening when you picked up that first cigarette.

C: We were out at a party, and a friend of mine was smoking, and I took one of his.

T: When you picked up that first cigarette at the party, were you planning on going back to smoking?

C: No, I was just going to have one. I know that you told me that I couldn't have one, but I really thought that I would have one that evening, and then never smoke again, but by the next day it was as though I had never quit at all. I guess I really made a mistake by trying that one.

T: You'll find that we look at everything in a positive way. I don't think we ever make any mistakes in our lives. So let's mark that first attempt up as a good learning experience, and we will make sure that the one cigarette does not sneak up and get you.

ANTICIPATION

Over the years I have heard the statement, "I can't wait until I reach my goal weight of pounds".

I understand that there is a certain amount of excitement about reaching your goal, but some times we tend to forget that anticipation can, and usually is the best part of the event.

As a child I can remember the anticipation of Christmas.

I used to say that the day after, the day after, the day after tomorrow is Christmas.

As a child every Christmas was wonderful, but no matter how great Christmas was, there was always more enjoyment in the anticipation of the event, than experiencing the event.

Even today as an adult, we may plan a vacation, and spend weeks, or months planning, and anticipating the vacation. After the vacation is over we may realize that we received as much or more enjoyment from the planning, and anticipation of the vacation as we did from the vacation it self.

So I do not want you to over look the enjoyment of anticipation that you can experience of these next few months as you progress on with weight loss. In fact you will discover that the anticipation of reaching your goal will be almost as enjoyable as reaching the goal it self.

Realizing that you will be enjoying the procedure of losing weight, as much as reaching your goal, will make this endeavor pleasant, and enjoyable.

BIG LOTTERY

It has always amazed me how easily we can alter the way we think about a certain figure.

I can recall a time when myself, and an associate of mine were running some errands. At this particular time the state lottery was up to over 40 million dollars.

I had never been that interested in the lottery, but for 40 million dollars, I drove out of my way to purchase lottery tickets.

As I was driving back to the office, fantasizing about 40 million dollars, it hit me.
Here I was making a special trip to purchase lottery tickets, simple because the jackpot was million. It seemed ironic that when the jackpot was only 10 or 15 million dollars, it wasn't worth
my time to drive a few miles out of my way.

Who would bother spending ten minutes of their time for a measly 10 million.

So often we become so involved with a large number that we tend to forget how great a smaller number can also be.

I have seen individuals in the past that may need to lose a hundred pounds or more, and they seem disappointed with only loosing 20 pounds in the first month or two.

In the same way that 10 million dollars is not as great as 40 million dollars, let's keep a positive outlook on each pound that you lose.

With each pound you lose, you are a winner.

DEEP SNOW

It seems so often that we allow outside stimulants to rule our lives.

We have all heard people say that the stress pushed me back into smoking, or the kids make me eat.

It is a lot easier to use another person or event as the excuse for failure, rather than accepting the fact that we have the ability to change the way we respond to any situation or events.

I can recall once a few years back when we had a terrible snowstorm.

One of the neighbors was out trying to get his car out of the driveway, and was cursing up a storm.

Another neighbor walked out on her porch, and said,

"I'm not going to make it to work today, but there was a good book that I have been wanting to finish.

Then there was n young boy who looked at all of that snow, and said, "thanks God", and jumped into the snow.

Each of these three people encountered the same stimulant. The snow really wasn't any deeper on one side of the street than the other.

One person viewed this-as a tragedy. Another thought "oh well". Finally the last individual viewed this as a blessing.

You too, can change the way you view any situation or circumstances, to ensure your total success.

DOG WITH A BONE

I would like to share with you a story. This is a story about a silly dog.
Although everyone loved this dog, there was one thing about him that no one could understand. It seems that this dog carried a big white bone in his mouth, everywhere he went.
Although the dog looked silly with that bone hanging out of his mouth, and it was truly an inconvenience for him to make sure that he always had his bone with him, he never went anywhere without it.

One day after a rain shower, the dog was walking down the street and happened to catch a glimpse of himself in a puddle of water. As usual he had that silly old white bone in his mouth.

It was amazing how he looked at his reflection, as if, maybe for one of the first times in his life, he was seeing himself as others see him.

That dog dropped the bone to the ground, and started to walk away. He only took a step or two when he began to head back to get his bone. He looked at his reflection without the bone in his mouth, and walked right past the bone never looking back again.

PERCENT OF LOSS

First you will be very pleased at how effectively you will be loosing weight after this session is over.

I would like you to do me a favor and change the way that you look at your progress.

In the past you monitored your progress by how many pounds that you have lost in a given time period. From now on, I would like you to think in terms of percents.

By that I mean calculate the percent of your loss, rather than pounds. For example, you need to loose fifty pounds, so once you have lost five pounds that is 10 % of your goal.

Ten pounds would be 20 % of your goal, and even two and a half pounds is still 5 % of your goal.

That sounds so much better than saying I have only lost   pounds.

You will discover that this will keep you motivated, and you will achieve total

In case you haven't already noticed we look at everything in a positive way here. So I want you to see your results in weight loss also in a very positive way.

Are you ready to start calculating your wonderful accomplishments in the weeks to come?

NO WILL POWER

You told me that you did not have any will power. Now, I do not believe that to be true.

Think about it. If a person did not have any will power they would not get out of bed in the morning, or go to work, or any of the other dozens of things that you do each day of your life.

So you have will power. You simply have not yet begun to use that will power in the area of weight loss.

Today you are going to learn to use that wonderful will power that you had all along.

Most of us have many abilities and talents, but that does not mean that we necessarily use them all.

Now that we both realize that you do have will power up there in that great mind of yours, are you ready to put it to work in the area of weight loss?

You may also discover other abilities that you had all this time, but have not been using them until today.

ELEPHANT

I would like to share with you a little story that illustrates how powerful our minds really are.

In this story a young boy went to a circus with his father. The young boy noticed a full-grown elephant that had a rope tied to his leg. The other end of the rope was tied to a wooden stake driven into the ground.

The young boy asked his father, "couldn't that big elephant pull that stake out of the ground if he really wanted to"?

The father explained, how when the elephants are just babies, they would attach a heavy chain to their leg, and hook that chain to an iron rod driven deep into the ground. The baby elephants would pull, and tug trying to get away, but they could not escape. The little elephants became so conditioned to failures, that now you could simply tie a cloth line around their leg, and hold it in your hand. Today as soon as the elephant feels the slightest resistance, he stops trying.

Now, we both know what would happen if that elephant ever gave it 100 % to get free, he would be gone.

Many times we as human being have failed so many times that perhaps we never honestly give it a 100 % to win.

Well, today you are going to give it 100 % one more time to accomplish   .

HEAR - SEE - FEEL - KNOW

There are some wonderful, positive things beginning to take place today.

You are now beginning to hear things the way an individual at (120 pounds) hears. You are now beginning to see things the way a person at (120 pounds) sees.
You are already beginning to feel the way a person at (120 pounds) feels.

Most important of all, you are now beginning to know, what a person at (120 pounds) knows.

Yes, you are truly beginning to hear, see, and feel the way a person at (120 pounds) hears, sees, and feels.

We both know what this means. You now have the ability to hear, see, and feel the way an individual at (120 pounds) would hear, see, and feel, you are becoming that person with the weight of (120 pounds).

GRANDPARENTS

You are a very intelligent person. You knew, just as I knew that some day you were going to become a nonsmoker once and for all.

You knew all along that you were not going to become an eighty-year-old (grandmother) sitting in a rocking chair, gasping away on a cigarette.

How ridiculous that would be.

So, it really has not even been a case of whether or not you were going to become a nonsmoker, but simply a matter of when, and how.

You have answered both of these questions here now today.

This is your day to become totally free, of that smoking habit. This is the day that you have chosen.

You are doing this for your own benefit, and personal well being, so this means that you can, and you will be successful as of today.

Never again will you need, or have to smoke.

FRIENDS

I would like you to realize a very important fact.

The two of us are here today for one reason, and one reason only. Think of it as two people working together for a common goal.

Think of it has two friends working together to become free of this smoking habit, once and for all.

Since we are friends working together, I would like you to make a mental decision that you are going to allow both your mind and body to respond to the positive suggestions that I will be sharing with you.

That's right, make a mental decision that you will allow your mind and body to respond to these powerful, wonderful suggestions.

Once you have made this mental decision, I would like you to simply nod your head yes, and relax even further.

We are now ready to move ahead to total, complete success.

RED

You will discover that after this session is over that the color RED will seem sharper, and more vivid to you than ever before.

Yes, the color RED RED RED will seem brighter and sharper to you than ever before.

Whether it would be a taillight, a stop light , color of a car, or clothing. It may be as small as a ladies nail polish or as large as a billboard, but the color RED RED RED will be more noticeable to you than ever before.

Each time your mind encounters the color RED, consciously, or subconsciously, your desire, determination, to reach a weight of 122 pounds can and will keep growing stronger.

Now, you will not need to look for the color RED, but you notice it automatically. It will be sharp, bright, and clear to you.

Each and every time your mind sees the color RED, consciously, or subconsciously, your desire, and determination to succeed will keep growing stronger.

Every suggestion, and instruction that I have shared with you today will continue working more effectively each time you see the color RED RED RED.

LICENSE PLATES

I would like you to realize that you see so much more than you ever give yourself credit for.

Throughout your daily activities you are seeing, and subconsciously evaluating millions of objects without being aware of it. Your subconscious mind is always alert, and is recording information.

Now, if the information is unique or unusual, then we become consciously aware of the object, or event.

I am sure that there has been many times in your life that you were driving down the road, and found yourself reading or analyzing one of those personalized license plates. It may have been a name or a unique abbreviation.

We both know that when you are driving your car, you are not consciously saying to yourself, I
will be on the look out for specialized license plates.

No, in fact you were not even consciously looking at any license plates initially. Your subconscious mind was evaluating, and recording everything that your eyes were seeing. Yes, regular, and personalized license plate alike.

When the subconscious mind encountered a unique license plate, it then brought this information to the conscious level of the mind, and then you consciously analyzed the plate.

So, yes we see much more than we ever realize.

THE ROAD RUNNER

So many times people tend to associate hypnosis, and the hypnotic state with what they see on the television, or in movies.

Although they may be very intelligent individuals if their only experience of hypnosis has come from television, and movies, they tend to say to themselves, I know it can't be that way but perhaps it is similar to what I have seen in the past.

This is only normal. If we do not have anything to compare hypnosis to, we would normally associate it with whatever past experiences that we have encountered.

I can remember one Saturday morning when I was sleeping in. My little girl came running into the bedroom, and said, "dad you have to get up. I have been watching cartoons, and the coyote is hypnotizing the poor roadrunner".

On the cartoon they showed spirals coming from the coyotes eyes, with the roadrunner looking all glassy eyed, saying, I hear and obey.

So even as young children our first contact with hypnosis usually has some type of a mystique surrounding it.

In reality hypnosis is a very normal natural state.

EAT A FLOWER

I would like you to spend a moment and imagine one of the most beautiful flowers in the entire world.

This perfect flower looks great. This perfect flower smells wonderful.

Although this perfect flower looks good, and smells good you would never consider eating it.

So yes, there will be foods that may look good. Yes, there may be foods that smell good, but that does not mean that you must eat them.

It is easy to see that there may be dozens of things in our life that look good, and may smell good that we would not consider eating.

The fattening foods, and or liquids are now falling into that category of objects that could look good, or smell good, but we will no longer consider eating them.

From this moment on, when you catch yourself saying, or thinking, that looks good, or smells good about a fattening food, you will think back to the example of the flower and have what it takes to say NO to eating it.

You will now be amazed and pleased with your new choices of foods, and liquids.

MONEY WASTED

You have been smoking two packs of cigarettes each day now for over 25 years. I wonder if you ever stopped to think about how much money you have spent on cigarettes over all of these years. All of the money up in smoke.

In reality it wouldn't do us any good to think about or worry about something that is already done.

The important issue would be to think of the future, and be certain that we would not make the same mistake again.

By becoming a nonsmoker as of today, it is astounding how much money you could be saving over the years to come.

In five years you could save over $6,500.00

In ten years you could save over $17,400.00

In fifteen years you could save over $34,700.00

In twenty years you could save over$62,600.00

In twenty-five years you could save over $105,000.00

In thirty years you could save over $180,000.00

No, matter what you decided to use all of that money for, we can be sure that it would be better than allowing it to burn up.

FIVE YEARS
ONE PACK EACH DAY

$ 3,250.00
TEN YEARS

$8,700.00
FIFTEEN YEARS

$17,350.00
TWENTY YEARS

$31,300.00
TWENTY FIVE YEARS

$52,500.00
THIRTY YEARS

$90,000.00

TWO PACKS EACH DAY

FIVE YEARS
$6,500.00

TEN YEARS
$17,400.00

FIFTEEN YEARS
$34,700.00

TWENTY YEARS
$62,600.00

TWENTY FIVE YEARS
$105,000.00

THIRTY YEARS
$180,000.00

THREE PACKS EACH DAY

FIVE YEARS
$9,750.00

TEN YEARS
$26,100.00

FIFTEEN YEARS
$52,050.00

TWENTY YEARS
$93,900.00

TWENTY FIVE YEARS
$157,500.00
THIRTY YEARS

NOTE: EACH OF THE ABOVE FIGURES REPRESENTS A 10% INTEREST ON THE BASSES OF $ 1.50 PER PACK. THERE IS NOT AN INCREASE PER PACK FIGURED INTO THE TOTAL DOLLARS.

STATE LOCATION

You do have a powerful memory.

This wonderful memory of yours has the ability to recall everything that you have ever seen, heard, felt, or read.

I know that most people say that they can't hardly remember what they did yesterday, let alone a month ago.

This is because they have not trained themselves to properly log information in the correct part of the mind.

I would like to share with you how effectively you mind has worked in the past. If I would ask you to point to the state of Texas on a map, you could do so.
However, if I asked you who taught you that information for the first time, you would most likely not know.

So, when you first learned the geographical location of the state of Texas your mind determined that it was important to remember where it was located, but it was not important to recall that Mrs. so and so taught you that information.

From this moment on, the information that you hear, read see, or experience will remain with you to be utilized in the future.

RETIREMENT TIME

T = THERAPIST C = CLIENT

T: I would like to get a little information about your smoking habit. T: How much have you been smoking up to this point?
C: About three packs a day.

T: Sounds like a professional smoker. If you are going to do something, you might as well do it right .

T: How long have you been smoking? C: Around 25 years now.
T: That sounds like retirement time for cigarettes, doesn't it? C: I think it is past time.

TIME SMOKING

T = THERAPIST C = CLIENT

T: How much do you smoke on a given day? C: About two packs a day.

T: Most of the time is you smoking or not smoking?
C: Without a doubt most of the times I have a cigarette at least burning in the ashtray.

T: I see, if most of the time you were not smoking, it would probably make it even easier to quit, wouldn't it?
C: I'm sure it would be easier.

T: Let's take a look at your smoking habit. You are smoking about 40 cigarettes a day. The national average for time smoking i8 five minutes per cigarette. 40 times 5 equals about
200 minutes of smoking or about 3 and a half-hours a day.

Let's see there are 24 hours in a day, and you are smoking just under 3 and half-hours out of those 24. That means that 20 1/2 hours each day you are not smoking.

I guess in reality most of the time you are NOT smoking, are you?

DEFECT

Now you have a very powerful mind. The most powerful part of your mind is the part that we call the creative mind.

The creative part of your mind may have worked against you in the past. This is the part of your mind that can generate some of the most sensibly, logical, and intelligent reasons why it is alright to   .

I am sure that you have caught yourself in the past, working on justifying why it is alright on this one day to go on and   .

As of this moment I want you to think of that creative part of your mind kind of defecting. That's right defecting to the other side. The side of you that truly needs, and wants to .

Imagine how effective you will be now, with that creative part of your mind now generating, positive, logical, and sensible reasons why you should   .

NOT LOGICAL

You have stated that it seems odd to you that you have not been able to quit smoking on your own.

Don't feel bad. First nicotine is one of the most addictive chemicals in the country today. In fact nicotine has been proven to be more addictive than heroin, cocaine, or liquor. It is not more harmful, but it is more addictive in nature that any other chemical.

Most people have tried to become free of the smoking habit by using their logical mind.

They say to themselves, these cigarettes are harming my health, they're dirty, they smell, socially unacceptable, and they will take time off of my life, right, right. I think I'll have a cigarette.

Smoking is an illogical habit. useful benefit in our lives. not serve any

So it is almost impossible to remove an illogical habit with logic.

Today you are tapping into the most powerful part of your mind. You are now using your own subconscious mind to become free of this illogical smoking habit.

LOOKS LIKE YOU NEEDED

T = THERAPIST C = CLIENT T: It looks like you needed that.
You did very well, you have an excellent concentration

You really do have a good mind. Wasn't that a wonderful feeling?
Tell me, at what point in the session did you realize that you were hypnotized, was it when you could not open your eyes, or when your hand started to float up in the air, or was it when you became aware of that numbness?

C: No, I knew something was taking place, when you were talking- about my body feeling relaxed. I realized early on that I was hypnotized, or something was taking place.

T: Are you ready now to give it all you have to be a success at? C: I am sure I will make it now.

NASTY

You are now ready to become free of this unwanted smoking habit once, and for all. For you, here, and now the whole idea of smoking is becoming so silly, and ridiculous.

In fact for you the whole idea of smoking is now, becoming so silly, and ridiculous that even the thought of it brings kind of a nasty taste to your mouth.

The smoking habit is now out of the past, and will never be able to control your life again. Free of that smoking habit. Free of that old nasty taste of cigarettes as of now.

It feels good to be a nonsmoker. It is good to be a nonsmoker. You are now ready for a new life as a nonsmoker.

SPECIAL CHAIR

T = THERAPIST C = CLIENT

T: Hello, my name is . T: Come on in to the office .

T: You can have a seat over here in the nice comfortable chair. That is our official stop smoking chair. There has be-n actually thousands of individuals that have stopped smoking in that very chair.

T: It sort of feels like a nonsmoking chair, doesn't it? C: I guess we will find out soon enough.

T: You are right. You will discover very soon how great it is to be a nonsmoker.

ALL YOU CAN EAT

As you have told me there tends to be times when you are at a buffet, and it seems almost impossible to control your food intake.

First, let me assure you that you are not alone with these feelings. There are many, many other individuals that used to view "all you can eat " as an open invitation to overeat.

Some people spent months, while other people spent years at allowing the buffet to control their lives.

In all of these cases where people used to be out of control when they entered an eating establishment that had all you can eat posted, they changed the way they viewed eating.

I have heard from so many people over the years that all of a sudden they started thinking about the buffet style eating as a cattle trough.

They report that each time they would stand at the buffet they would think about a herd of cattle pushing, and shoving trying to keep eating.

It didn't take to long before the idea of all you can eat became so disgusting that they would always pass on the buffet.

HAMMER

The key to all types of behavior is to be in control of your own actions.

Most people encounter a stimulant, and then respond immediately to that stimulant.

If I were hammering a nail into the wall, and I missed the nail, and hit my thumb. I would have definitely encountered a stimulant, pain.

Now, normally we might throw the hammer down,, kick the wall, and say a few choice words. That would be the response.
If we would add a third step to our behavior, and add analyze, we would then be in total control. So, we hit thumb with hammer, and encounter stimulant pain. We now analyze our options,
throw hammer across room, kick wall, curse, or perhaps run some cold water over the thumb. By
adding the third step of analyzing we may create a new alternative response.

If after analyzing all options we chose to kick the wall, this would be an acceptable response, simply because we chose to react in this manner, rather than the pain controlling our lives.

BINGES

Many people who have experienced binges before, feel that they will always be bingeing. In some cases that may be true.
For what ever the reason may be, some people have a natural tendency to binge, when it comes to eating.

You may in the past found yourself bingeing on sweets, salts, snacks, or another type of food.

You will continue this bingeing, even after this session is over. That's right you will continue on bingeing after the session is completed.

However you will discover that the binges will now be changing. There may be a week or two that you tend to be bingeing on carrots.

The very next week, you might discover yourself bingeing on water. Down the road the binges might be directed towards apples, or some other type of food.

You will have a large selection of food to select from, for your binges. You may choose from fruits, water, vegetables, or ice.

This will be a behavior that will be both satisfying, and rewarding for you.

60 SECONDS

You have been doing very well, and you will continue to relax even further now.

In just a moment I am going to give you 60 seconds without the sound of my voice. During that
60-second period, many positive thoughts will come and go through your mind. The next time I speak to you, you will be twice as
Begin this 60 seconds now.......

60 SECONDS LATER

That was very good. It is sort of amazing how many thoughts can come, and go through your mind in just 60 seconds. Yes it has been just one minute, and your mind has created many, many different thoughts without any conscious effort.

Today this same response will begin to work for you in the area of   . Yes, if you are capable of generating many thoughts in one minute imagine how many positive thoughts, plans, and strategies that you could create throughout your daily activities.

With this unique, powerful part of your mind working for you, it is obvious that you will be a total, and complete success in
    .

TODAY'S DATE

Today is May 10th 1987. This is your day.

Throughout your life, you have always managed to do wonderful things for other people. You have been someone's daughter. You have been someone's wife, and mother.
You have been someone's secretary, and someone's friend or neighbor.

Today is your day. This is the day that has been selected to take care of yourself.

Today, May 10th 1987 is becoming just as important as any birthday, holiday, or anniversary. This is the day that you are becoming free of the smoking habit once and for all.

This is your day, and it will continue doing wonders for you in years to come. This day of May 10th 1987 is well past due.

You will be very thankful that you have spent the time here to make these wonderful changes in your life.

You will always remember this day of May 10th 1987 as the day that you took time' for yourself, and became free of the old smoking habit.

WORD OF HONOR (IDEO)

IDEO MOTOR RESPONSES

Will every part of your mind and body make a promise to work with you, in allowing you to become a non-smoker?

WAIT FOR YES RESPONSE

May I now have your word of honor that you will never again allow cigarettes to control your life?

WAIT FOR YES RESPONSE

Will you now give your word of honor that you will never again take a single puff, drag, or draw from a cigarette?

That's good enough for me.

WAIT FOR YES RESPONSE

WORD OF HONOR (MENTAL)

As you continue relaxing even further now, I would like you to make a promise.

This is not a promise to me, or to another member of your family. This is a promise to yourself.

In fact I would like you to actually give your mental word of honor that you will now become a success at.

That's right, give your mental word of honor that you are now ready to take control of your life. Once you have given this mental word of honor, I would like you to simply, nod your head yes, and relax even further.

Now, without a doubt you will become successful at

Not because I say so, but just simply because you have given your word of honor, and you are a positive, trustworthy individual.

Already you are feeling good about this decision. This positive feeling will continue growing stronger with each passing day.

ADULTS ARE CHILDREN GROWN TALL

It is amazing that children have the ability to create and remove habits easily. One day a child may create a habit of whistling; the next day the habit is gone. The child may then create a habit of skipping; a few days later that habit is gone. So yes, children have the ability to create and remove habits easily. Adults are simply children grown tall. There is still a bit of child in all of us. So, we can use that childish ability to remove negative habits and behavior patterns that are no longer useful for us. You have abilities that you have never even begun to use. One of those abilities that you do possess is the ability to forget. Forgetting is an ability that is not alien to anyone. We actually learn to forget as a way of keeping our conscious mind from being cluttered with unneeded, unwanted information. We may hear a joke or, a story and even say to ourselves, " That was good. I will remember that". And yet somehow two days later, we have forgotten it completely.

So forgetting is an ability that we can actually use. You are now beginning to forget. Forget the thoughts and ideas of smoking. Smoking is something out of the past. We no longer need it today. We can forget and let it go.

10 STOP SIGNS

With your eyes closed I would like you to picture your hands at your side. Once you have this image of your hands in your mind, I would like you to nod your head yes.

WAIT FOR RESPONSE

Very good, now I would like you to imagine an image of your hands, and fingers. In your imagination you are beginning to create an image of your fingertips.

In this image instead of finger nails at the end of each your fingers, and thumbs, I would like you to imagine small red, and white stop signs.

That's right ten little stop signs instead of your fingernails. Get this image clearly imbedded in your mind.

From this moment on if your hands, or fingers begin to move up to your mouth with the intention of biting your nails you will become aware of the movement, and , over your hands to another location.

Anytime your hands would start towards your mouth to bite, chew, or pick at your nails, you will think about this image of the ten small stop signs.

The stop signs mean STOP. This is precisely what you will do. You will totally stop biting your nails. You will allow them to grow longer, and healthier.

This is occurring because you are ready for it now.

SENSITIVE ARM

I would like you to begin to recall a time in your life that you felt uncomfortable. It may have been a time when you felt out of place, or embarrassed.
It may have been a time when you felt self-conscious.

As you begin to recall that time, I would like you to nod your head yes.

WAIT FOR RESPONSE

That's good. Now I am going to say five different words to you, and as I do you will begin to feel some of the uncomfortable feelings from the past.

Number one. CHOCOLATES. Feel those uncomfortable feelings again. Number two SODAS. The feelings become stronger with each word. Number three. COOKIES. Uncomfortable, not enjoyable.
Number four CANDY. The feelings growing even stronger.

Number five ICE CREAM. The feelings are becoming just as strong as they were in the past, and the things that have brought back these feelings are.

Chocolates, sodas, cookies, candy, and ice cream.

Just hearing about chocolate, sodas, cookies, candy, and ice cream makes you feel uncomfortable.

These are now foods, and liquids that you no longer need or want. They no longer can, or will allow you to feel good.

Now say the following words after me, and notice how that uncomfortable feeling returns.
Chocolate   Soda   Cookies
Candy   Ice Cream

Anything that could , or would make you feel this uncomfortable is something that you will truly avoid.

CHANGING SIDES

NOTE: THE FOLLOWING TECHNIQUE IS CONDUCTED WITH AN IDEO MOTOR RESPONSE.

T = THERAPIST C = CLIENT

T: The part of the mind that has been causing you troubles with   ,
has that part of your mind been doing so for some time now?

WAIT FOR RESPONSE

T: In the past, years gone by did that behavior seems like the right thing to do?

WAIT FOR RESPONSE

T: Would that powerful part of your mind that has been causing you these problems now stop interference, and actually trade sides, and begin working even harder in reverse to help you become free of   .

THE MUSIC IS GONE

NOTE: WITH THIS TYPE OF KEY PHRASE IT IS PREFERABLE TO USE MUSIC THAT WILL PERIODICALLY FADE IN AND OUT DURING THE SESSION.

You may not have even noticed consciously, or sub-consciously when or how the music faded away, but it has.

The music has faded away with or without your conscious knowledge, or acceptance, and it is gone. The smoking habit is fading away with conscious knowledge, and acceptance so it to has gone forever.

In just a moment I will be bringing you back to a fully alert state, where you will feel rested, and refreshed.

BOWLING

I would like you to spend a moment and think about the game of bowling. Bowling like many they games, or sports has the object of seeing how high an individual is capable of scoring.

In bowling a perfect score would be 300. Bowlers strive to reach the perfect game of 300 as the final outcome.

If having 300 written out on their score sheet was so important why don't they simply fill out the score sheet with a 300 score, and not bother working at it.

The reason is very evident, the joy of reaching a 300 game is obtained through some effort. Simply having a score sheet with 300 written on it would not be enjoyable. with weight loss, we sometimes forget that we can actually enjoy the challenge of striving for our goal almost as much as reaching the goal itself. You will enjoy striving for pounds.

WORKING OUT

You will find that some of the things that I suggest to you will seem quit different from other things that you have heard in the past.

You told me that you have an exercycle that has not been used now for a number of years.

I would like you to start a policy of ridding that exercycle for a minimum of 30 seconds each day. That doesn't sound to hard does it?

I know you are thinking, 30 seconds won't help me.

I assure you that by exercising for a minimum of 30 seconds everyday, you will be amazed at the difference in your overall well being.

I call this plan, DOWN GRADING TEE GOAL TO THE RIDICULOUS LEVEL.

The hard part is not ridding the cycle. The hard part is throwing your leg over it, and making the first revolution.

You will discover that 99 time out of 100 you will ride it longer than 30 seconds will. This way we eliminate the excuses such as, I don't feel good, not enough time, and so on. This 30 seconds will continue to grow.

THE FUTURE

From time to time we mentally travel back in time, to recall an event from the past. Today you are going to do the exact opposite. Today you are going to be traveling forward in time.

I would like you now to travel forward in time with me, and imagine yourself in the following way.............

Think of yourself with the weight of your body at or around   pounds. Imagine yourself with your personal life in order.
Begin to think of yourself with your private life totally content, and at ease.

Your family life is pleasant, and wonderful, and you are in better physical shape than you have ever been in before.

As you think of yourself in this way, and in this way only, you are realizing that there is no food or liquid anywhere in the world that could compare to turning this image of your future into a reality.

You will always eat enough food to keep you alive and well, but you will never need, or have to over eat again.

THINKING

The time has come for you to become free of this old, unneeded smoking habit.

The smoking habit is now becoming something totally out of the past. There is no longer any need to allow smoking to control your life.

In fact from this moment on, you will hardly ever even be thinking about cigarettes again.

If, you would happen to be thinking about cigarettes again, you will be thinking about how much better feeling as a nonsmoker will.

You will be thinking about how much better you will be looking as a nonsmoker. You will be thinking about how much better your whole life has become.
You will be thinking about how wonderful it has been to use your own mind to wipe out the smoking habit forever, and ever.

SHOE TAP

In just a moment you will begin to feel, and hear a slight tap on the bottom of your left shoe.

As you begin to hear, and feel this light tap on the bottom of your shoe, you will begin to experience a wave of relaxation, moving up through your left foot, and leg.

Now, as I tap your right shoe, notice how the right foot, and leg also relaxes. As I continue tapping on your right show, experience that relaxed feeling moving upwards, into your right hip, and the right side of your stomach. A tap on your left shoe now creates a relaxed feeling on your left hip, and stomach. Feel that relaxed feeling moving up through the left side of your chest, neck, and head. Now, the right side of your chest, neck, and head. Your right hand and arm, relaxed. Your left hand and arm relaxed.

Your entire right side of the body relaxed. Your entire left side of the body relaxed. Your entire body relaxed, and at ease.

From the bottom of your feet to the top of your head, both the right side, and the left side of your body is relaxed, comfortable, and at ease.

JUNK FOOD

I am sure that you have seen or heard of the association test.

This is where a single word is said, and you say the first thought that comes into your mind.

Today we are going to conduct this test in a different way. I am going to say a word, but instead of you telling me what word pops into your mind I would like you to create an image in your mind. Later on, I will try to guess what type of images came to mind.

Let's begin now.

The word is junk. Junk, think of junk. The word is again junk. Think of all types of things that are junk.

I am now going to say several things that you may have been thinking about, when I said the word junk.

If one of my guesses is correct, simply nod your head yes, and relax even further.

Old cars rusting away. Old parts that no longer serve any useful purpose. Outdated magazines, or newspapers. Useless objects of no value. Certain types of food.

I guess we both know the true meaning of junk food, and why to avoid them now;

CHILD INDUCTION # 1

I am going to touch the bottom of your feet. As I touch the bottom of your right foot, I would like you to let that foot go to sleep. Now, I am going to touch the bottom of your left foot, and let the left foot go to sleep.

Now, it is time for your legs to go to sleep. Go to sleep legs. Your tummy is going to sleep. Your chest is going to sleep. Go to sleep tummy, and chest.

Your hands are now going to sleep. Your arms are going to sleep. Good night hands, and arms. Your neck is going to sleep. Your head is going to sleep. Even your eyes, nose, and mouth are all going to sleep,

Everything except your ears is going to sleep. Your ears are staying awake, so that you can hear me.

I am going to lift up each of your feet. When I let them go they will flop back to the chair, because they are a sleep.

Now, I am going to lift up both of your hands, and when I let them go, they will also flop back down to the chair.

Now, every part of your body is a sleep.

FEAR - NOT EXITING

Over the years I have had many people say to me, that they have heard about wonderful results with the use of hypnosis, but they were afraid that they might not come out of it.

Once I was doing a gentleman in his mid seventies. He asked me the question, what if I am hypnotized, and you had a heart attack and died.

He really wasn't worried about me having a heart attack, he wanted to know if another hypnotist came by, could they bring him out.

Now, today I am not planning to have a heart attack, but if you were in the deepest level of hypnosis, and I decided that it was time for me to go home, and I left you there, which I would not do. What would happen to you, in four to five minutes of me no longer talking you would simply fall asleep, and wake up once you were rested.

If someone came into the room and shook your arm, you would wake up instantly. The only time people stayed hypnotized his when they are doing it on the late show.

FEAR TELLING

T = THERAPIST C = CLIENT

T: One of the things that I hear from clients each week is, what if I tell you something that I
didn't want you to know.

First of all you are not going to be volunteering any information today, and secondly, you could even lie when you're hypnotized.

I get this question from husbands, and wives. Would it be all right if I came in during the session, and asked my spouse a few questions?

It seems that most people think of hypnosis in the same way that they think of the lie detectors, or truth serum. In reality they are not related at all.

For sake of example, I am going to ask you a question, and I want you to lie to me. Have you ever had a glass of water?
C: No.

T: I didn't think so. See, even in this abstract example, the correct answer comes into your mind, but you have the ability to say whatever you wish.

FEAR - CONTROL

Now, you may have read or heard, that you can not be made to do anything under hypnosis that you do not wish to do.

This is a true statement.

If you were in a very deep level of hypnosis, and I said, I WANT YOU TO GO OUT, AND ROB EVERY BANK IN THE WORLD, AND BRING ALL THE MONEY BACR TO ME, AND THEN WASH MY CAR.

You would instantly, pop open your eyes, say no, and walk out of the office.

You see that with hypnosis a person never looses control. They do the opposite. They begin to take control of a part of their lives that perhaps they did not have control over before.

Doesn't that sound great.

HYPNOTIZED YES NO

T = THERAPIST C = CLIENT

T: Now, there may be moments during this session when you mentally say to yourself, I wonder if I am hypnotized or just relaxing. It doesn't appear to be like what I have seen on television.

I would like you to simply keep an open mind. Sometime during or after the session I will ask you.

Do you think that you have been hypnotized?

At that point you can once again use your logical mind, and make a decision.

Up to that point just wait and see. You will be amazing yourself with abilities that you have never discovered

Are you ready to experience hypnosis now? C: Yes ...

MIND WANDERING

THE FOLLOWING HAS BEEN PROVEN SUCCESSFUL IN ALLOWING THE CLIENT TO REALIZE MIND WANDERING IS A NORMAL PART OF THE HYPNOTIC SESSION.

During the session you may find times where you feel as though you're not even listening to me. Your mind may have wandered off on all different types of thoughts.
Do not let this disturb or distract you. You will still be gaining full benefit from the suggestions that are given

So if you find your mind wandering from thought to thought, simply let it go. You will do great.

ALMOST ASLEEP

Today, during this session you may feel as though you were right on the verge of falling asleep.

In fact there may be moments when you say to yourself, doesn't he/she ever stop talking. If he/she would be quiet for just a moment I would fall a sleep.

You don't need to worry, I am never quiet. I talk 11 hours a day.

In fact the joke among friends is, he/she took a breath, hurry up and say something. So don't worry I'll keep you awake.

You will not only be awake but, you will hear everything that I say, and remember everything that takes place. The sensation will be close to how you feel at night just prior to entering sleep.

You are laying in bed, but you can still hear sounds in the house, or perhaps traffic out on the road, but you are totally relaxed. That is how you are going to feel when you are hypnotized.

THE WATCH

Although your subconscious mind has amazing abilities, it does not have the ability to analyze. The subconscious takes everything literally.

For example if we could communicate verbally on a subconscious level and I asked you, "do you know what time it is"? Your response would be, "Yes"

If I then asked, "would you tell me what time it is"? Your response would now be, sure I would be willing to do that.

Finally I would have to say, WHAT TIME IS IT? Oh, it is   .

Normally, if I passed you on the street and said, excuse me do you know what time it is? This time your analytical mind would go through the following thoughts.

He must not have a watch. He would like me to look at my watch, secure the time, and verbally pass that information on to him. That seems safe enough.

Since the subconscious can not analyze, many times we reach for food, cigarettes, or other negative behavior when in reality, we may have been searching for a totally different type of need. The want may have been companionship, reduce stress, or overcome boredom.

NOT COMPARED TO

I would like you to travel forward in time with me. Imagine yourself now with the weight of your body at, or around   pounds.

Think of how wonderful you will be looking at   pounds. Imagine how great you will be feeling with the weight of your body at   pounds.

Now there may be a food or liquid that looks good. There may be a food that even smells good. But, not compared to you at weight of pounds.

In fact we both realize that there is not any fattening foods or liquids, anywhere in this world that could compare to that positive weight of pounds.

You will always eat the amount, and types of foods that your body needs to keep you healthy, and strong.

The fattening, high calorie foods can no longer compare to the enjoyment, the excitement, and the pleasure that you will be deriving from reaching, and maintaining a weight of pounds.

ANYONE WITH NORMAL

In almost every conversation one individual is trying to determine what the second party will be saying prior to them speaking.

In hypnosis, there is a set of questions, and predictable responses that all hypnotherapists have encountered many times before.

Listed below is the way that the questions usually flow.

John, Can everyone be hypnotized? Therapist; Oh, yes anyone can be hypnotized. John; I'd bet that I can't be hypnotized.
The last statement by John is almost a certainty. He has tricked the therapist into making a commitment that anyone can be hypnotized, and then made a challenge, I'd bet that I can't be hypnotized.

Now let's examine the new way of answering the question, can anyone be hypnotized? Your response will now be ...

Yes, anyone with normal intelligence can easily be hypnotized.

If John would be foolish enough to say, I'd bet that I can't be hypnotized. Your response might be, maybe your right.

3 MINUTE RULE

The one thing that most of us that are either overweight, or that have ever been overweight have in common, is that we tend to be sort of compulsive.

That simply means that there are times in our lives, when we have made a decision and later on we wish that we would have waited.

Many people, have experienced purchasing an item from a store, and then a week later, they wished that they would have waited on it.

When it comes to making purchases, the rule is give it seven days. If after seven days the item still has the appeal that it once had, then you can be sure that it is something that is important, or needed.

Now, if you were considering eating a cookie, we both know that you are never going to wait a week to see if it was important to you.

This is where the THREE-MINUTE RULE comes in. If you were tempted to eat a food that is not beneficial in helping you reach, and maintain a weight of   pounds, I would like you to give it three minutes before eating that food. Half of the time you will totally forget about the food, or become involved with another activity. Then there will be other times when it is no longer important to you. Either way, you will be winning.

THE BOOKS

I would like you to imagine yourself walking down a long hallway. At the end of this hallway, there are two double doors.

As you approach these two double doors, you are wondering what will you find inside.

You reach the doors, and swing them open. Inside you see that both the right, and the left side of the room is filled with bookshelves. Then you also notice that the right side of the room has thousands of books on the shelves, while the left side has only a few books scattered on the shelves.

As you walk into the room, you pick up one of the first few books on the right side of the room. As you open the book, you realize that this book is about a happy, positive moment in your life, one that has just recently occurred. It may have been coming here today.

You walk halfway down through the room, and pick up another book from the right side of the room. Once again this book seems to be about another happy time, about midway in your life.

You now proceed all the way down to the end of the room, and pick the last book on the shelf, from the right side of the room.
As you open that last book, you discover that this is a story about your own wonderful birth. Everything is now making since. The books at the end of the room, are about happy events early
in your life, and the books, near the door, are chapters of the most recent part of your life.

The one thing that is still puzzling is that every one of the books that you had looked at was a wonderful, positive parts of your life. There were no negative stories at all.

Then you glance over to the left side of the room, where there were a few books scattered on the shelves.

You realize that these must be the negative events. You spend a few moments trying to decide whether or not to open any of these volumes. Finally you decide that since you are here, you might as well take a look at what has be causing you for all of these years.

You walk over to the left side of the room, and begin to look for a book titled, THE CAUSE OF
                              .   .

You see that title on the second shelf. You pull down that book, and open it to the first page. You
          now understand what has been giving you all the problems in   .

You instantly, rip the cover of the book off. You notice that there are several trashcans there on the left side of the room. However, there is not a single trashcan on the right side of the room.

It is obvious that it is alright to destroy this negative chapter from your life, and start fresh. You rip every page out of the book, and toss it in the trashcan.

The moment that you threw away that last page of that book, it is began to feel as though you could smile on the inside and out, both at the same time.

You leave this room knowing that you can, and will be successful at   . You will now be adding only positive volumes to this collection.

KITCHEN TABLE

You have told me that the majority of times when you are eating, you are eating in front of the television.

I have had clients over the years that almost convinced themselves that eating near the television would improve the reception.

One of the things that I would like you to do for me as of today, is to implement the policy of eating only at the kitchen table. There are several reason why this will make a dramatic change in your life.

First, imagine yourself sitting in front of the television watching a good movie, and the thought pops into your mind, we have chips in the cabinet. You get up, bring the bag of chips into the other room, and continue watching the movie. Sounds like fun, doesn't it?

Now imagine the same situation, but this time you sit down at the kitchen table, and eat chips. It really doesn't have the impact that it once had.

The other advantage is, that you can't feel deprived with this system. Basically you can have almost anything you want. The only stipulation is that you eat that food at the kitchen table. You will never find yourself saying, poor me I can't have any because I am loosing weight. Since you wont feel deprived there is nothing to give up on.

INVESTMENT

You are very happy that you made the decision to use hypnosis in order to be successful at

These last few moments have truly been an enjoyable sensation, one that you will remember in a positive way for the rest of your life.

In fact, to you, these last few moments honestly have been one of the best investments of your life.

You are now becoming an inspiration for both men and woman alike.

What a wonderful feeling that is. You may not ever know how many people that you directly, or indirectly have helped by your own example.

What a wonderful feeling to help yourself and others at the same time.

REJECT

The time has come for you to take control of your own life, and eliminate these unneeded, unwanted eating habits. Reaching, and maintaining a weight level of   pounds is rapidly becoming the priority in your life.

You have a right to reach, and maintain a weight level of   pounds. You have what it takes to reach this goal quickly, and safely.
In your case it is not a lack of knowledge.
You know what you should be eating, in order to reach a weight level of   pounds. Today you are going to begin using all of the knowledge, wisdom, and experiences that you have stored within your own powerful mind.

It is a fact that you have talents, and abilities that you have not used in a number of years. However, any ability that has been discarded by your conscious mind can be rejuvenated now. At this very moment you are now analyzing, and reviewing all of your past abilities.

You have known all along what needed to be done in order to ensure your success at reaching, and maintaining a weight level of   pounds.

The time has come now, this very moment to initiate these new healthy eating habits.

One of the new abilities that you do have is the ability to REJECT things, thoughts, and items.

I am sure that there have been times in your life that you were looking for a new shirt, or other item of clothing. You may have even pulled it from the rack, and then decided to reject it for one or more reasons.

There have been thousands of items, and thoughts that you have rejected.
The ability to reject is the ability that is going to ensure your success at reaching, and maintaining a weight level of   pounds.

You are now rejecting the thoughts of sugars, and sweets. You are now rejecting the thoughts of overeating.
You are now rejecting the old ideas, that you must finish everything on your plate.

You are rejecting, any and all thoughts of eating for other reasons other than true hunger. You are now rejecting all thoughts of being overweight.

SMALL CLOTHING

NOTE: THE FOLLOWING IS TO BE USED DURING THE PRELIMINARY SESSION.

T = THERAPIST C = CLIENT

T: So, (CLIENTS NAME) you are now ready to eliminate this excess weight once, and for all?
C: Oh yes, I have a whole closet full of clothing that is too small for me. T: That's great ! I love hearing that statement from my clients.
That means that you knew all along that some day, some how you were going to get down to   pounds.   If you knew, or believed that you were always going to be overweight, you would not kept all of those nice clothes. You would have given them away, sold them, or threw them out.

So part of your mind must have known all along that it wasn't a question as to whether or not you were going to lose weight, but simply when.

Well you are now answering that question here today.

Are you ready to eliminate that excess weight once, and for all? you are now answerin8 that question here today.

C: Yes ...

DIABETIC

You may know, or heard that diabetics must stay a way from sugars.

There are thousands of diabetics in this country that have found the ability to stay a way from sugars, simply because they need to.

You have a dramatic advantage over the diabetic. Yes, it is true that you also need to stay a way from the sugars in order to reach, and maintain a weight of   pounds.

The advantage that you have is not only do you need to become free of the sugars, but this is also something that you WANT to do.

You are doing this for your own benefit, and your own personal well being. You are becoming free of the sugars as of today.

You will continue to be very pleased with the decision that you have made. This will benefit you from this moment on, for the rest of your life.

TYPEWRITER

Over the years I have had hundreds of people tell me that they really did not feel that their activity level has changed at all over the years, but their weight level continues to increase.

There was a research project conducted a few years ago that took a secretary that normally typed
6 hours each day. They were able to determine that if she went from a manual typewriter, to an electric typewriter, she would gain 3 pounds over the next year. Now, that is under the premise that nothing else changed in her life.

At first we would not have felt that something that simply would create such a difference. With the electric typewriter, she no longer had to push the carriage return, there was no effort exerted in feeding the paper, and she applied less pressure on the keys.

If we begin to analyze just a few of the many changes that have taken place over the years, it is easy to see how our activity level has truly reduced.

In today's time most of us have the luxury of automatic transmissions, power steering, and air conditioning in our cars. At home we now use remote controls for the television, a cordless phone that keeps us from having to move too much, and many people have electric garage door openers.

These are just a few of the many items that we have all become accustomed to over the years. Rapidly almost every activity is becoming push button. Now, one of these items would not cause

a problem, but when we begin to combine all of the activities that have been eliminated in our daily lives, it is easy to see where the problem stems from.

Should we eliminate the conveniences, and appliances from our daily activities?

No, we should appreciate the remarkable advances that have taken place over the years, but at the same time we need to accept the fact that each of us will need to make a more conscious effort to become more active.

ONLY ONE COOKIE

I would like you to imagine a little girl about 5 or 6 years old.

This little girl asks her mother if she could have a handful of cookies. The mother says, "no, you may have one cookie".

The little girl is upset, but takes that one cookie to the table. She spends a few moments looking at the top of the cookie. Then she spends sometime looking at the bottom of the cookie, and even the sides of the cookie.

Finally she takes the smallest little bite of the cookie, and lets it dissolve in her mouth.

Then a second bite, and finally after many bites and about ten minutes of time, she takes the last tiny bite of the cookie.

She picks up a few crumbs that had fallen onto the table, pops them into her mouth, and let's out a sigh of satisfaction.

It is quite evident that this little girl received much more enjoyment from that one cookie than she would have from even a dozen cookies.

Now, if a 5 or 6 year old child has enough wisdom in her life to eat less and enjoy it more, surely we as adults could do the same.

ORDER AT A RESTAURANT

It seems difficult sometimes for people to refrain from having seconds, or thirds when it comes to eating.

Even if we took a large helping initially, it is so easy to come back for more.

The interesting thing is if, we were at a restaurant, we would order what we wanted, and be satisfied with the quantity of food in front of us.

I wonder how often you have ordered food at a restaurant, finished the meal, and then ordered a second or third meal.

No, we don't order additional food, when we our out to eat.

From this moment on I would like you to respond to a meal in the same way you would at a restaurant.

You will select the type of food, and the quantity of food that you need. The food that you place on your plate will be your meal. Set in your mind that whether you are at home, or away, you will predetermine the quantity of food that you will be eating, and you will then respond in the same way that you have always responded at.-.a restaurant.

Only one meal. Only one helping.

Safely, quickly, and comfortably you will be reaching a perfect weight of   pounds.

LIPSTICK

I know that your wife is still a smoker. That's alright there are many things that your wife may use that you do not need, or use.

On a daily base your wife may use lipstick, nail polish, mascara, eye shadow, perfume, and cigarettes.
So, there are many items that your wife may choose to use, that would have no bearing on you. You are your own person. You have the right and the ability to select what you will be doing. From this moment on. There is no person, thought, idea, memory, image, feeling, or sensation, out of the past, in the present, or ever to arrive in your future that could trick you back into that old smoking habit again.

You are now totally, completely free of this embarrassing smoking habit.

THE PRESIDENT

You will discover that I will not ask you to do anything that you are not capable of doing. I will not ask you to imagine yourself in a situation that would never occur.

For example I would have you imagine yourself as an astronaut, simply because I really do not think that you will ever become an astronaut.

I would not have you think of yourself as the president of the United States. It is possible, but I
doubt that you are ever going to become the president of the United States.

So we understand that only the type of images or thoughts that I will have you create are images and thoughts of things that will definitely occur.

Now, spend a moment with me, and create an image of yourself with your weight at or around an image of   pounds.

Get this image clearly imbedded in your wonderful, powerful mind. This is an image that will shortly come true for you.

It is alright to think of yourself at   pounds. This is a true image of your positive future.

3 GODS

There is a fable that I once heard that illustrates just how powerful our minds really are.

There were three gods that were trying to decide where to hide the greatest power in the universe, where man would not be able to find it, and use it destructively.

The first god said, " I know where to hide it, let's hide the greatest power of the universe on top of the highest mountain, man will never think to look for it there".

But it was decided that some day man, might climb the highest mountain, and discover this power.
The second god said, " let's hide the greatest power of the universe at the bottom of the sea". Again it was agreed that someday man might explore the bottom of the sea, and thus discover the
greatest power of the universe.

Finally the third god said, "I know, let's hide the greatest power of the universe in the mind of man, they will never think to look for it there".

So according to the fable, the three gods hid the greatest power of the universe in the mind of man. Now, although this is a fable, our minds have the greatest power of the universe.

DRUGS

You asked me earlier if you should keep, or throw away your cigarettes. Let me ask you, do you have any heroin in your purse?

Of course not. The reason that you do not have any heroin in your purse is because that is something that you are not going to use today, and it is something that you do not plan on using in the future.

Basically the only thing that you keep on you is things that you will be using today, or things that you plan to be using in the near future.

Since you will not need, or have to smoke, there is no longer any reason for you to have cigarettes with you.

As you throw them away, you will feel as though some great, heavy burden has been lifted from you.

You are now in control of your own life, and actions. Enjoy this new positive feeling.

100% EFFORT (SMOKING)

T = THERAPIST C = CLIENT

T: Tell me have you ever really tried to quit smoking before? By that I mean giving it a true
100% .
C: Yes once I quit for just over three months.

T: That's good. Are you ready to give it 100 % today with hypnosis? C: Yes ...

T: Tell me have you ever really tried to quit smoking before? By that I mean giving it a true
100 %
C: No. I have never really tried before.

T: You are very honest. Are you ready to give it that 100 % today? C: I am ready.

3 CATEGORIES (SMOKING)

Allow me to explain what you are going to be experiencing after the session is over. People usually fall into one of three categories.

About 30% of the people I see report that it is almost as though they never smoked at all. They never really think of cigarettes again. Doesn't that sound great? Put you down for that one right.

The second category, with about another 30% will not have any craving for a cigarette but may experience an automatic reaching. For example the telephone may ring and you reach for a cigarette, and then realize, I don't smoke anymore. The thought will fade away almost as quickly as it entered your mind.

The third category, with another 30% may have a little bit of a mind battle going on. I think I would like to have a cigarette with this cup of coffee, piece of pie, YES ... NO ... YES ... NO ... Give it just a couple of moments and it will fade away.

You could handle anyone of those three categories, couldn't you?

FOURTH CATEGORY

T = THERAPIST C = CLIENT

T: Let me tell you about my failures, since you are not going to be one.

I'll get a call, and they say IT DID NOT WORK. I ask, what didn't it do?
The response is almost always the same, I left your office, went out my car and lit a cigarette.

I tell them, well it sounds like you wasted   dollars and an hour of my time.

Honestly, if you said I changed my mind, and I don't want you to hypnotize me, I am going to really try to quit on my own. Well surly you could make it a couple of hours wouldn't you agree?

C: Oh, I could make it at least a day.

T: Of course you could, so the person who walks to the parking lot, which takes about two minutes, and lights a cigarettes, did not try very hard. They could have done better than that without me.

They went into this with the attitude, "YOU CAN 'T MAKE ME QUIT' '. Then they go to car and light up a cigarette. I can not make you quit smoking, but I can help you dramatically.

WHAT IF?

I would like to share with you the two most dangerous words in the world. They are WHAT IF?

Yes, we can use these two words "what if" and begin to worry about something that might, possible, you never know could happen.

By using these two words we can create a tragedy for any day of our lives.

What if I went home tonight, and my spouse handed me a rose. What if the rose had a thorn on it. What if I pricked my finger. What if the finger became infected. What if I couldn't find a good doctor. What if they then had to amputate my arm What if I was now driving with only one arm. What if I got into an accident. What if a piece of glass from the windshield cut my vocal cords. What if I could never talk again. I would be out of business. I'm not going home tonight.

This is an abstract example of what iffing, but it does show how important it is to eliminate those two words from our daily lives.

A $ 5.00 CAR

It seems so often that we tend to forget why, we are devoting effort to a certain task.

No matter how much an individual may enjoy their job, there would not be to many people showing up for work if the company made a statement that they were no longer paying wages.

So the amount of the reward must be equal to or greater than the amount of effort given. Sometimes in weight loss we tend to forget what we will be receiving for the effort that we are giving.

If I offered to sell you any car in the world for $ 5.00, that would be a bargain. Now, surely you would not be driving home from here in your new car, and be complaining that you no longer had your five-dollar bill.

The reason that you would not have any complaints with this exchange, is that you would feel like you gained much more than you gave.

When you reach a weight level of   pounds, you will feel better, you will look better, your confidence will grow, and you will begin to like yourself more.

All of these benefits, and rewards for simply becoming more selective in the foods that you eat.

In reality, the amount of effort to reach your goal is very similar to the five-dollar car. You are receiving much more than you are giving.

HEALTH CLUB PAYMENT

Wouldn't it seem silly to have a nice house that you are paying for each month, but never live in it.

Imagine a person that would buy a new car, but instead of driving it they left it parked in the street.

How about someone that would go out to a clothing store, and purchase several new outfits so that they could hang in the closet never to be worn.

I am sure that we both agree that all of those actions would be ridiculous, and not thought of. What a waste of money that would be.

You are now beginning to realize how silly, how ridiculous it is for you to have paid for a membership that you are not even using.

You would never buy a new outfit, and not ever wear it. You would not even think of buying a new home, for the purpose of leaving it vacant.

So the idea of having a membership in a health club, and not using it on a regular basis is now becoming something out of the past.

You have made the decision to move ahead in your life, this is for your own benefit your own well being.

TIME DISTORTION (TEST)

You have really enjoyed these last FEW MOMENTS very much.

You are beginning to feel as though the last COUPLE OF MOMENTS have been the best investment of your life.

Although you have only been hypnotized for a FEW MINUTES today the results will remain with you forever.

NOTE: FOR BEST RESULTS THESE SUGGESTIONS SHOULD BE DELIVERED TO THE CLIENT JUST PRIOR TO HAVING THE CLIENT EXIT THE HYPNOTIC STATE.

AFTER EXITING ASK THE FOLLOWING QUESTIONS.

Off the top of your head, a brief response how long do you think you were under, if you were just going to take a guess in minutes?

IF THE TIME DISTORTION WAS MORE THAN DOUBLE THE CLIENTS GUESS TELL THEM THE CORRECT AMOUNT OF TIME, AND EXPLAIN THAT THIS IS A NORMAL REACTION FROM A PERSON THAT HAS BEEN HYPNOTIZED.

IF THE GUESS WAS TO CLOSE TO THE TIME, SIMPLY STATE, GREAT YOU HAVE A EXCELLENT MIND.

SAYING THE ALPHABET

T = THERAPIST C = CLIENT

T: Over the years I have had many individuals that have experienced trouble in understanding the difference between conscious, and subconscious.

To help you have a better understanding of the two parts of the mind, I would like conduct a little experiment with you.

In a moment I am going to have you recite the alphabet as quick as you possibly can, while I time you.

Begin now.

C: a b c d e f g h .... z

T: That was very good. Now let's do it again, but this time I am going to make it easier on you. I am going to have you say only half of the alphabet, and I'll time you again.

T: This time when I say go, I would like you to say every other letter. C: Laughter
T: Yes, it would now take you much longer to accomplish half of the job. That is because this time you would need to think about each letter, consciously. The first time you responding subconsciously. Can you now see how much more effective the subconscious is?

TIME WASTED

You have many good reasons for wanting to be a non-smoker. I would like to share with you a very good reason to eliminate the smoking habit forever.

You can always earn more money. There are many times that our health can be restored, but the one element of our life that we can never add to is time.

You may never stop to think about how much time you have spent smoking.

For example an individual that smokes 1 1/2 packs per day for twenty years has spent over one million minutes smoking. That calculates to 18,250 hours of smoking or 760 full days of smoking, or just over 2 years of your life smoking 24 hours a day every minute of the day for two years.

It is time to save our precious time and stop smoking NOW.

RELAXED ATTITUDE

First let me assure you that you are not alone with the habit of coming home in the evening, and overeating.

For one reason or the other many people have developed the habit eating, the moment that they walk in the door. Some people contribute this behavior to a feeling of it is now time to relax, take care of me, and begin an evening of eating. The first part of that feeling is correct. It may be time to relax, and take care of yourself, but we do not need to include an evening of eating.

From this moment on, you will begin to experience a relaxed attitude, when you come home in the evening.

In fact you will soon be developing a relaxed attitude about eating.

You have worked hard all day. You have the right to have a relaxed attitude. You have the right to have a relaxed attitude about eating.

After working all day, the last thing you need to worry about is constantly going back to the icebox or cabinet.

You should not have to work on eating once you are home in the evening. So a relaxed attitude about eating, is becoming more appealing to you.

You deserve to have this attitude. You will enjoy this attitude. You will benefit from this attitude.

BECOME THE BEST DRIVER

You will be pleased to learn that today you will not hear any negative suggestions, or statements from me.

Many people have experienced stop-smoking programs that would attempt to scare them into becoming a nonsmoker. The theory behind the scare tactic is, this will shock the smoker into quitting.

As you may have already experienced, the scare tactics do not work. The thought is to show you a picture of an old black lung, and say this is what your lungs look like. You are expected to look at the photo, and say oh my God I will never smoke again. If the photo was extremely disgusting, you might cut down for a day or two, but you most likely would not quit.

I know that if I am driving down the road, and see a bad traffic accident, I then become the best driver in the world, for about the next 5 miles. Then we forget about the fearful situation, and slip right back into our old habits.

Today, and from this moment on, you will be concentrating on the positive benefits of being a nonsmoker, rather than the negative consequences of smoking.

ASPIRIN

Many people who are ready to change their eating habit, and, begin to loose weight, really are not sure how they should be responding to food.

There are still others that may know what they should be doing, but have trouble in accepting the fact that they have the ability to make correct choices.

Regardless of how you felt before, it is now time to take control of your own life, and realize how much control you always had.

For example if you had a headache, you might take an aspirin. You would not even consider taking a half of a bottle of aspirin, or perhaps taking heart medication in place of the aspirin for a headache.

If you felt fine, you wouldn't take anything.

So, when it comes to medication, you have the ability to take the type that is needed, the quantity that is needed, and only when it is needed.

You are now going to begin the process of relating these same abilities over to your eating habits. Eating only the type of food your body needs, in the quantity that it needs, and only when it needs food.

THROW AWAY FOOD

First, let me assure you that you are not alone when it comes to feeling guilty about throwing out left over foods.

Thousands it is to people in of individuals grew up hearing about how sinful waste food. Many of us heard about the poor in China that are starving to death.

Sometimes we say to ourselves, that there isn't enough to save, and I hate to throw it out, so I'll just finish it off.

I would like you to use your imagination with me. Let's pretend that I have a magic button. If I would push this magic button you would instantly reduce down to a level of   pounds, and stay there.

Now, if I told you that I would push this magic button if you would go home, and throw away
$100.00 worth of good food, we both know what you would do.

Although it might seem like a waste to throw out $ 100.00 worth of perfect food, you would do so if you could instantly reach a weight of   .

I do not want you to go home and throw away food. What I would like you to do is the next time there is a little of this or that left over, and you begin to mentally battle whether or not to throw it out or eat it, think back to this example. You will remember that you were willing to throw out
$100.00 in food. That small amount of leftovers will never equal the $ 100.00, but it will lead you to the same point of reaching   pounds.

LARGE PACK

You have many good reasons for wanting to be a nonsmoker. It is going to improve your health. It will allow you to breathe easier. You will be saving thousands of dollars in years ahead.

However there is another very important reason to become free of this smoking habit. No one wants to be controlled by another individual. So, it is only natural that no one would want to be controlled by an object.

Up to this moment cigarettes have been controlling your life. They have been telling you what to do.

Imagine for me a large pack of your cigarettes, about three-foot tall. Now, think about that pack of cigarettes with hands, and arms, feet and legs. It has a face right on top. It is the face of the person that you dislike the most in the world, maybe a pushy type of person.

Think of that large pack of cigarettes pointing it's finger at you and saying, "I know that you wanted to quit smoking, but I can control your life".

You don't want to hear this, you don't need to hear this. Notice how that large pack of cigarettes is now changing.
The hands and arms are fading away. The feet and legs are vanishing. That head, the face of the person that you dislike the most is now leaving.

The entire pack of cigarettes is now beginning to shrink, and fade away. It is becoming smaller, and smaller. Fading away, fading right out of your life.

That pack of cigarettes is now becoming so small, that you can just barely imagine it, protruding beneath a blade of grass.
You now want to make certain that these cigarettes can never come back and tempt you again. You want to be certain that those old cigarettes will never come back and tempt anyone that you care about.

Imagine taking your foot, and smashing that pack of cigarettes down into the ground so far that it will never come back again.

Once you have totally destroyed the cigarettes and the smoking habit forever, nod your head yes, and feel good about what you have accomplished.

SHOT GLASS

I am sure that you have heard how important it is to drink water while you are loosing weight. Many people find it difficult to comprehend drinking six, to eight glasses of water each day. We are going to make it easier for you than ever before to drink the water you need.
I would like you to put a shot glass by your kitchen sink. The type of glass that you use in mixing drinks. The glass only holds an ounce.

Now, instead of pouring liquor in the shot glass, I would like you to take a shot of water each time you walk by the kitchen sink.

You will amaze yourself at how easy, and simply it will be to consume a large amount of water, without really working at it.

Although you will now be establishing this new policy of taking a shot of water each time you walk by the kitchen sink, do not discontinue your normal water drinking.

In fact you may notice that not only will you be drinking water with the shot glass, but your desire for water throughout the day will also increase.

This will be fun, enjoyable, and extremely beneficial to you, all at the same time.

THE BEACH

I want you to imagine yourself walking down a beautiful beach. There are several things different from this beach from any other beach in the world.

One of the things different from this beach, is that on this beach there is not any pollution. Everything is beautiful. On one side of you is the beautiful water, while on the other side are flowers, trees, and vegetation.

The other thing different from this beach is that you are the only one on this beach. That means you can be yourself. There is no need to pretend or to act. So often when we walk down a beach that is crowded with others we have a tendency to hold our stomach, and stand a little straighter.

Today you can be yourself.

As you think of yourself walking down this beach you notice that a young child has written the numbers from 5 down to 1 in the moist sand. Perhaps with a stick. these numbers have been written for you.

You go up to the number 5, and lightly slide your foot across the number 5. the number 5 fades away, and you relax even further. You are not sure exactly how, or why this happens, but you wonder could the same thing happen to you again. You go to the number 4, and once again you slide your foot across the number 4, it fades away, and you relax even deeper again.

You are now beginning to feel as though you have discovered something wonderful. You go to the number 3, and this time as you begin to slide your foot across the number 3. The water comes in, and just touches your toes. The water does some of the work for you, and you relax further again.
You spend a moment now and, look back at the beach. You remember where once there was the number 5, the number 4, and the number 3, now the sand is smooth, and flat. However, you feel as though you have only done things half way. You do not want to do things half way.

You go down to the number 2, and as you begin to slide your foot across the number 2, the water comes in, and covers your toes. The water does most of the work for you, and you relax even deeper again.

You are now feeling great. As you begin to slide your foot across the number 1, the water comes in all the way up to your ankles. The water now does all of the work for you. The number one fades away, and you relax further again.

Once more you look back at the beach. You remember that on the number 5 you put forth some effort, and the number 5 faded away. You relaxed further.

You did not stop simply due to effort. You continued on to the number 4. Once again you put forth the effort, and the number 4 faded away. By the time you reached the number 3, the water came in, and did some of the work for you .

By the time you reached the number 2, the water was doing most of the work for you.

By the time you reached the number 1, the water was doing all of the work for you, and yet you relaxed even further.

It is amazing how similar that it can be in our daily lives. We begin the initial effort, and as we do things they keep getting easier, and easier.

MEMORY 2

All of us have had the experience of watching a game show on television where the contestants were asked various questions, and had to give correct answers.

As we sit in the comfort, and security of our own homes we are able to recall answers to the questions that the contestants on the show are unable to answer.

Do we have a better memory than the individual on the show? No, we are simply more relaxed, surroundings.
It is time for you to take those comfortable feelings with you, and use them whenever, and however you wish.

TAKE A BREAK

Over the years I have been amazed at how many people tend to associate a relaxing feeling with substances that actually are stimulants.

Many people say that cigarettes, coffee, or candy help them relax, and unwind. In reality all three of these substances tend us more stressful, or hyper.

So why do so many people associate relaxing with chemicals that are stimulants?

More often than not, we find ourselves falling into the habit of associating objects with taking a break. For example we have all heard statements such as, It is time for a coffee break. A cigarette break would be nice. I am going to take a break, and grab something to eat.

Many times what is happening is a person may feel that he or she needs to justify why they are taking a break.

If I worked for you and said, "I have really been busy, would it be alright if I took a break, and had a cup of coffee"?

Or perhaps the request would be, would it be all right if I took a break, and grab a candy bar? Then there is, would it be alright if I took a short cigarette break?
Each one of these three request seems almost normal to us. It seems logical to take a break and overdose on sugar, caffeine, or nicotine.

Now if I asked, "would it be alright if I took a break for a few minutes, and did absolutely nothing, maybe just stare out of the window"?

Your response would be, do you feel ok, is there anything wrong?
What is wrong, is that we have forgotten that we do have the right to take a break, and allow our minds, and bodies to relax, without the association of sugars, caffeine, or nicotine.

From this moment you will think of breaks, relaxation, and taking care of yourself in a new way. No longer will you associate   with relaxation, or taking a break.

TRAY OF GLASSES

Today you are ready to lose weight with the help of hypnosis. As you are well aware of weight loss is one of the most complex behaviors that people encounter, but with your determination and the aid of hypnosis you will reach, and maintain a weight level of   pounds.

One of the amazing things that you will discover today is that hypnosis will help you in the area of becoming free of the old behavior of giving up.

I am sure that you have experienced before the routine of doing well at loosing weight, and then you went off of the program one time, and it seemed impossible to get back on track.

It is almost as if we said to ourselves, well, I already ate that cookie, so I might as well

Conversational Hypnosis and NLP

have the ice cream too.

Weight loss is the only behavior that when we make a mistake we punish ourselves by eating the wrong foods again.

Wouldn't it be silly if we were carrying a tray of glasses, and one of the glasses fell off, and broke if we simply turned the tray up side down, and said, well, I might as well brake the rest of them.

How would it be if we were backing the car out of the driveway, and bumped into a telephone pole, if we said, now I guess I'll wreck the front of the car too.

These examples seem silly. However in the past you may have responded in the same way in regards to your eating habits. So if you find yourself using a mistake as a reason to give up, think back to these examples of the tray of glasses, or denting the car.

You will realize that it is no longer acceptable to give up, simple because of a mistake.
In fact IF you would happen to slip, and select a food or liquid that you really did not need in order to reach a weight of   pounds, you will simply become even more determined than ever to win.

FASTING

As you have shared with me earlier, the main problem with your eating habits, tends to be from to   .

Today we are going to eliminate these negative times in your life.

No, we can not remove the hours from to the clock, but we can change the way we respond to those time periods.

I do not want you to do this, but if I asked you to totally fast for 24 hours, I am sure with a great deal of effort you could do so. Yes, it could be done, but I do not want you to fast for 24 hours.

If I asked you to fast for 12 hours, you could fast for 12 hours with a certain amount of effort. I do not want you to fast for 12 hours.

So, we both know that if I asked you to fast for 6 hours that would take a very small amount of effort. I do not want you to fast for 6 hours.

Without a doubt, if I asked you to fast for 3 or 4 hours, you could do that without hardly any effort. I do want you to fast for 3 to 4 hours each day.

From   to   I would like you to begin a fast.

Each evening from   to   I would like you to totally fast from all foods, and liquids, with the exception of water.

DRIVE THRU

Today you are using the creative part of your mind to establish new, and healthy eating habits that will remain with you for the rest of your life.

You will begin to notice a cycle of improvements that will become progressively more evident to you with each passing day.

For some people these new ways of responding to food to be quick, and automatic, while with others they to be in a gradual, and progressive.

Regardless of how, or when the changes begin, they will be extremely beneficial to you.

A past client related a situation to me that shows very well how the creative part of the mind operates.

He and his wife were driving down the highway, and his wife made the statement that she was hungry. He said they would pull off the highway, and go to the drive-thru window of a fast food establishment.

His wife ordered what she wanted, and asked him, aren't you going to get anything? He replied, No, !'m not hungry. His wife then said, but we are here.

My past client shared with me how normally he would have said to himself, since I am not hungry, I'll have a regular hamburger, small fries, and a medium soda. I am not hungry. This time however, he realized that he could enjoy the company of another person but did not need to eat simply because they were eating.

It was as if, someone finally turned the lights back on, and he was able to see this improper eating habits for the first time in his life.
You too, will begin to see that the way that you respond to food beginning to change in a positive way.

Your eating habits will be changing in order to meet the requirements of your new body, at a new weight of pounds.

No longer will you be associating eating, with boredom, depression, time of day, other people, stress, reward, or companionship.

From this moment on, you will be eating only the foods your body needs, in the quantity that your body needs in order to ensure your success at reaching, and maintaining a weight of pounds.

ICE BOX

As I am sure that you are well aware of, most of us tend to reach for food for many reasons besides hunger.

I know that if I would get home in the evening before the rest of the family, one of the first things that I would do, is open the icebox.

I don't know if I expected to see them folded in two on the second shelf. No, I was starting to reach for food for companionship.

It would seem silly to sit on the couch, watching television with our arm around a watermelon. Yet so often we use food as a replacement for human companionship.

Once we start to realize that we are eating because of boredom, depression, time of day, other people, stress, reward, or companionship, we are then capable of creating a new way of responding to the food.

Almost everyone has found a time when they thought that they were hungry, and went to the icebox, or cabinet. They ate a few bites, and said, no, that's no it. Maybe it was something salty that I was looking for.

In reality, what they were looking for, had nothing to do with food. From this moment on you will not confuse other feelings with hunger.

SUPERIOR

You will be very pleased with your new life as a nonsmoker.

In fact, seeing other people smoking will have no bearing on you at all. You can still enjoy the company of other people who smoke, but you will not need or have to smoke yourself.

When you see other people smoking, it will make you happy that you no longer smoke.

If you are associating with other people who smoke, it will make you proud of the fact that you are no longer controlled by cigarettes.

From this moment on when you see other people smoking, whether you know them or not, may be just passing them by it will make you feel kind of superior.

Not necessarily that you are better than they are, but you realize that you have countered this smoking habit once and for all.

You will never need, or have to smoke again.

FIRST DATE

T: I would like you to begin to recall a happy, pleasant time in your life. I would like you to begin, and recall one of the first few dates you ever went out on.

It may have been to the movies, it might have been to a dance. It may have been a church or a school function, or simply a walk.

As you begin to recall back to one of those first few dates, I want you to nod your head yes, and relax further.

Good, now as I touch your right hand, don't allow the sound of your voice to disturb you, but instead allow it to help you relax further, like a deep dreaming state.

Tell me, where did you go on one of those first few dates or so? C: I went to a high school dance.
T: About how

C: I was sixteen.

T: I would like you now to begin, and recall even what you were all wearing back then. Over the years the styles have come, and gone. Sometimes they have come back, and sometimes they have never left.

As you begin to remember what you were all wearing back then, nod your head yes, and relax.

Tell me what were you wearing back at that time in your life. C: A full skirt, a sweater, and bobby socks.
T: That was fashionable back then, wasn't it?

C: Yes, that is how everyone dressed back then.

T: Tell me, if you were going to go to a dance tonight, 1990, do you think that you would dress the same way you did back them?

C: Laughter no, t am afraid I would look silly.

T: So, in the past that was the right thing to do. In the past is was alright, but in the present or in the future it would seem sort of silly.

In the past it may have seemed alright to smoke, but in the present, and in the future it would be totally ridiculous.

REFRAMING

NOTE: AFTER ESTABLISHING IDEO MOTOR RESPONSE,[1] PROCEED IN THE FOLLOWING MANNER.

The part of your mind that has been causing you to   , has that part of your mind been doing so for what it felt or believed was for your own benefit or good?

Now the creative part of your mind. The part of your mind that has the abilities to come up with new ways of doing things. Would that part of your mind now be willing to help you become free of?

Would the creative part of your mind now accept the responsibility of coming up with five (5} new healthy ways of responding instead of   ?

Can you, will you, now begin to start those new healthy strategies, and become totally free of?

Is there any part of your mind that has an objection to these new five (5) healthy ways of responding?

Are any of these new ways of responding dangerous, or harmful to you in any way? Good allow them to begin now.

REFRAMING (CONSCIOUS)

NOTE: T = THERAPIST I.M.R = IDEO MOTOR RESPONSE

---

1 Ideo motor is most commonly used in reference to the process whereby a thought or mental image brings about a seemingly "reflexive" or automatic muscular reaction, often of minuscule degree, and potentially outside of the awareness of the subject. As in reflexive responses to pain, the body sometimes reacts reflexively with an ideomotor effect to ideas alone without the person consciously deciding to take action. The effects of automatic writing, dowsing, facilitated communication, and Ouija boards have been attributed to the phenomenon.

T: Would the creative part of your mind allow you to begin a habit of thinking, and reaching for water in place of sweets?

I.M.R. Yes.

T: Would the creative part of your mind allow you to begin thinking more about walking, and exercising? I.M.R Yes.

Would the creative part of your mind now be willing to allow your metabolism to speed up to a healthy rate? I.M.R. Yes. REFRAMING (CONSCIOUS) CONTINUED

Would the creative part of your mind now assist you in eating slow less food? I.M.R. Yes. thus become full, and satisfied with

Would all parts of your mind, and body now begin working together as a team to ensure your success at reaching, and maintaining a weight level of lbs.? I.M.R. Yes.

Is it trues that everything you tell me has to be the truth? I.M.R. Yes
Now that we realize that everything that your creative mind says, is the truth. Will you now make a firm promise that you will ensure (CLIENTS NAME) success at reaching, and maintaining a weight level of   pounds?

I.M.R. Yes.

FAN INDUCTION

As you continue listening to my voice, you will soon notice yourself slipping into a wonderful, relaxed hypnotic state.

You will discover that all tension, and stress will be pouring right out of your body. Every muscle tendon, and ligament will keep relaxing further, and deeper.

In a moment I am going to begin to count back from ten down to one.

As I count back you will begin to experience a soothing cool flow of relaxation covering your entire body. It might first be experienced in your feet and legs. You may notice this cool wave of relaxation beginning in your shoulders. Regardless of where you experience this sensation first, it will be pleasant, and enjoyable.

As you begin to feel this cool wave of relaxation, let yourself slip into an even deeper hypnotic state.

Ten, let yourself go. Nine, deeper, and more relaxed. Eight, what a positive feelings. Seven notice the changes. Six (turn on fan) feeling relaxed, and at ease. Five that's right, let yourself go. Four, still deeper, and deeper. Three, more relaxed than ever before. Two, you are even amazing yourself. One, that's it.

THUMB & FINGER

NOTE: THE FOLLOWING POST HYPNOTIC S WGESTION IS DIRECTED TOWARDS THE INDIVIDUAL TNAT IS PRIMARILY KINESTHETIC IN NATURE.

You are now ready to eliminate this excess weight. You are now ready to reach, and maintain a weight level of around, or about   pounds.

I would like you to spend a moment for me, and lightly rub your thumb, and index finger together. Do this for me now.

(WAIT FOR CLIENT TO RESPOND) Good.....
As you lightly rub your index finger, and thumb together, you are beginning to notice a very pleasant secure feeling. A feeling of confidence. Now, before you would eat or drink any food or liquid, I would like you to just lightly rub your thumb, and index finger together, and simply allow these wonderful feelings to return.

You will be relaxed, and in control of your eating.

SPORTS CAR

There are many, many things in our lives that are always changing. The one area of our lives that constantly changes, is the way we think.
It has always amazed me that when a certain situation was going on, and a particular thought or feeling was 8enerated we have a tendency to think that we will always feel the same way.

Some feelings or thoughts will automatically change themselves with time. Other thoughts or feelings can be changed at will.

I can remember as a teenager growing up, how impressed, and envious I was when I saw some one driving a new corvette.

Today when I see some one pulling into the parking lot with a new corvette, my thoughts are, I feel sorry for them with that high car payment, and outrageous insurance.

No longer do I feel envious, but instead I feel grateful that I am not tied down to those high costs. So yes, our thoughts can change completely.

TELL THE TRUTH

T: From everything that I have read, and my years of experience has shown me, what you tell me now must be the truth, is that right?

C: Yes response.

T: Good, now will you become a nonsmoker as of today? C: Yes response.
T: Will you now be a nonsmoker for the rest of your life? C: Yes response.

ACTOR

As you well know, actors, and actresses rehearse over, and over again so that when it comes time for the actual performance they will respond in actually the same way that they have rehearsed.

The more frequently an individual rehearses the better the performance will be.

All of us have encountered this same proven theory in our daily lives. It might have been at work, or around the house.

I am sure that there has been occasions when you mentally planed or rehearsed how you were going to respond or accomplish a certain task.

Today I would like you to mentally rehearse how you are going to respond to eating.

Imagine yourself at home, or away and being in control of the foods, and the liquids that you consume.

Think of yourself being tempted to slip back into that old negative way of eating, but instead of giving in to the temptation rehearse the new way that you will be responding.
Imagine someone offering you some type of sweets, and this time you are saying "no thank you". Think of yourself being tempted to reach for food because of boredom, stress, anxieties, time of day, or other people. Now mentally rehearse your new response of saying no, to that thought or temptation.

Each night prior to falling asleep rehearse the way that you want to respond in regards to your eating habits.

TEN STORES

I would like you to understand how important it is to select, one, and only one location with in your household that you will eat at. The best location would be the kitchen table.

The average person has at least four or five separate locations with in the house that they routinely eat at. It may be the kitchen table, the living room, or family room. Some people find themselves eating in front of the icebox or at the counter.

It is a proven fact that if you would decrease your eating to only one location you would also dramatically decrease your overall food intake.

Imagine going Christmas, or birthday shopping, and you travel to ten different stores. There is a strong likelihood that you would spend more money purchasing a few items at ten different stores, than you would have by confining your shopping to a single store.

The same holds true, in regards to our eating habits.

If we stay with a single location within the home to eat at, we will automatically, easily and permanently, decrease our food intake.

THE COFFEE TASTER

I would like you to imagine a young man in his mid-thirties. This man is a professional coffee taster.

Think of this individual sitting at a table with several cups of coffee in front of him. Now imagine him picking up one of the cups of coffee, and spending a few moments to notice how the light reflects off the surface of the coffee.

He now spends a few more moments totally enjoying the wonderful aroma of the coffee.

Only after enjoying the sight, and the aroma of the coffee does this professional coffee taster allow a few drops of the liquid to touch his lips, and tongue. He then savors the delegate taste of the coffee.

Now, compare this professional coffee taster to the person that would be sitting in an old coffee shop, slurping down the cup of coffee so quickly that he really did not even have a chance to enjoy the sight, the aroma, or the taste of the coffee.

Just as drinking coffee that can be an art, eating can also become an art by learning to eat properly.

From this moment on, I want you to spend a few moments to appreciate the sight of the food that you are about to eat. Enjoy the wonderful aroma of the food, and most important of all, take small tiny bites of your food.

Bite thoroughly, and completely.

You will become full, and satisfied with far less food than it used to take.

MAGIC BUTTON

T: You told me that you really were not sure if you wanted to quit smoking or not.

I am going to help you decide if this is or is not what you want to do.

If I had a magic button, and all you had to do is push the button, and you would instantly become a nonsmoker, would you want to push the button?

C: Oh, yes I would push it in a second.

T: Of course you would, and this means that you really do want to stop smoking once, and for all.

So often when I hear someone say, "I am not sure if I really want to quit or not", what they are really saying, is "I am not sure-that I can quit."

There is part of our minds that finds it easier to say I did not want to rather than I could not do it.

Are you ready now to get rid of this smoking habit, as of today?

GIFT AS A CHILD

NOTE: T: = THERAPIST C: = CLIENT

T: I want you to recall a time as a little girl when you received something very special. It may have been a beautiful dress, or a special doll. As you begin to recall a special time as a young child when you received something very special, I would like you to nod your head yes.

Good, now I am going to touch your right hand, and as I do tell me about that special item. (TOUCH RIGHT HAND)

C: It was a pretty dress.

T: Did you get that dress for a special occasion? C: Yes, It was for Easter.
T: About how old were you then? C: About six years old.
T: Tell me, were you a cute little girl back then at age six? C: Well kind of cute.
T: Did you smoke back then at age six? C: (LAUGH) NO, not back then.
T: Wouldn't that have been ridiculous, seeing you at age six coming out of the bedroom in that beautiful Easter dress, with a cigarette hanging out of your mouth.

C: (LAUGHING) Yes it would have.
T: Honestly it seems kind of ridiculous to be smoking at anytime in your life, doesn't it?
C: Yes it does.
T: In fact the whole idea of smoking is now becoming just as silly, just as ridiculous, JUST AS UNTHOUGHT OF as it would have been at age six. Would this be ok with you?

C: Yes it would.

CHANGING THE EVENT

THE FOLLOWING IS VERY EFFECTIVE IN REMOVING A NEGATIVE IMPRINT, OR THOUGHT FROM THE PAST.

T: = THERAPIST C: = CLIENT

T: As I touch your right hand, I want you to begin to experience the same type of feelings that you first experienced when your mind determined that you should be overweight.

It may have been a sad feeling, It may have been a lonely feeling. It may have been a frightening time. As you begin to feel those same feelings coming back as I touch your right hand, nod your head yes.

(WAIT FOR CONFIRMATION, AND PROCEED) T: Now tell me what kind of a feeling that was for you.
C: A feeling that I was not wanted.

T: I am now going to count from three down to one. On the count of one, you will see an image of your face at the age this feeling first began. One, the feeling is growing stronger. Two, you are starting to see an image of your face the age when you first felt unwanted. Three, you are now seeing an image of your face at the age that this feeling first began.

As you begin to see, or imagine this image, nod your head yes. T: How old were you then?

C: About seven or eight.

T: What was happening that made you feel as though you were not wanted? C: M   y mother is yelling at me.

T: What was she saying.

C: That I am too much trouble, and that some times she wishes that I never would have been born.

T: I want you now to imagine as though you could see that seven or eight year old (CLIENTS NAME) across the room. Now I want you to imagine being able to talk to her with all the knowledge, and wisdom that you have developed over the years. Convince her to trust you. Once you have that young (CLIENTS NAME) convinced that she can trust you, I want you to say the word yes out loud.

Good now I want you to squeeze my right hand. As you squeeze my right hand, I want you to imagine giving that little (CLIENTS NAME) a hug. Hold her close to you. Give her all of the love, and understanding that she has been missing. Give her the feeling of being needed, and wanted. The two of you are now coming together. You have her, and she has you. Feel all of the love and caring beginning to flow between you. Once that little (CLIENTS NAME) knows that she will have you forever, the hug begins to fade.

Her tears begin to stop. A smile replaces the look of hurt. The two of you have now found each other.

T: No longer do you need to turn to food for comfort.

You now feel as though a great heavy burden has been lifted from you. It is beginning to feel as if you could smile on the inside, and out.

NOTE: AT THIS TIME YOUR SCRIPT WOULD NAVE A POSITIVE EFFECT ON THE CLIENT.

MEMORY

NOTE: AFTER HYPNOSIS HAS BEEN INDUCED PPOCEED IN THE FOLLOWING WAY.

In just a moment I am going to say a couple of words or a phrase, and as I do it will bring back different pleasant thoughts. Each time a new thought or memory comes into your mind,

I want you to lift up one of the fingers on your right hand.

I want you to begin and recall a very pleasant time as a child. A day in school. It might have been the first day of school, it may have been the last day of school. It might have been a time going to or coming from school. Now as you begin to remember a time in school, lift up one of the fingers on your right hand.

Now I want you to recall a pleasant time as a child. A time playing in the water. It might have been a time when you were swimming. It might have been a time in the bathtub, or playing with the hose. It may have been a day during a rain shower. As you begin to recall this enjoyable time playing in or around water, lift one of the fingers on your right hand.

(WAIT FOR RESPONSE)

NOTE: THIS IS THE TIME TO HAVE THE CLIENT BRING BACK THE SPECIFIC MEMORY THAT YOU WERE LOOKING FOR. PROCEED IN THE SAME MANNER AS BEFORE. IF YOU WOULD LIKE TO HEAR THE INFORMATION ABOUT THE MEMORY, SIMPLY GIVE THE FOLLOWING SUGGESTION:

In just a moment I want you to tell me about that   time. You will now be able to speak to me and, the sound of your own voice will not disturb or distract you in any way. Now remaining relaxed, and at ease, tell me about this   time.

LEARNING THE ALPHABET

I realize that it may seem difficult to imagine yourself learning to live without

.

However, throughout your life you have learned and mastered many things that originally seemed almost impossible to learn.

As a young child, just starting out in school it seemed to be an almost impossible task to ever learn all of the letters of the alphabet.

There were so many different shapes.

Today of course if I would say to you the letter S . Without hesitation, or even thinking about it, you could imagine how the letter S is shaped and how it sounds.

The task that you are undertaking today is simply one of many tasks that may have seemed difficult or impossible in the beginning, but as time went on, it became increasingly easy for you to respond.

You will even surprise yourself, at how rapidly you will be mastering life without

.

NEED TO, HAVE TO

T: Do you want to be a nonsmoker? C: I need to.
T: That's good that you need to, but the important question is do you want to.

T: We have both encountered many things in our lives that we need to do. Things that we should do, or things that we have to do.

This however does not mean that we will do them.

We could walk out into the parking lot, and I could show you my car. Your response would properly be, that it needs to be washed.

I would agree that it needs to, it should, and it has to be washed, but guess what, I don't WANT to wash it, so it probably will not get washed.

We are better off wanting to accomplish a task than needing to. So, do you want to become a nonsmoker?

100% EFFORT (WEIGHT)

T: Tell me, have you ever really seriously tried to eliminate this excess weight in the past? By that I mean giving it a 100% .

C: Yes, I lost about 45 pounds a few years back.

T: That is very good. Are you ready to give it a 100 % today?

C: Yes, I'll give it everything that I have. I really want to get rid of this excess weight. T: That's great, there is no way to fail.

PROBLEMS WITH SCALE'S

You will shortly be loosing this unwanted weight, but I would like you to refrain from getting on the scale to often.

Many times a scale can be more harmful to us, regardless of what it says.

If we get on the scale and it says that we have lost a great deal of weight, we can use that as a justification to over indulge

If the scale says we have not done as well as we have hoped, we can use that as the reason to quit, and give up.

You will not need a scale as a guide to how wonderful you will be doing. You will notice the improvement in the way that your clothing fits, and how your energy level is increasing.

If you feel that you must check in with a scale DO NOT get on the scale anymore than once every two weeks or so.

If we could simply forget about the scales, and on our eating habits, the weight would take care of itself.

EVIL HYPNOTIST

I would like to share with you a simple definition of what a therapist would call an imprint.

Imagine for a moment that you went to an evil hypnotist, and he told you under hypnosis that you must be overweight.

Then you went to a good hypnotist, that's me, and I told you that you would lose weight.

You would then have two completely different thoughts in your mind, working against each other.

Now, of course you did not go to an evil hypnotist, but many people have a negative thought that may be working against them on their desire to achieve success.

Everything that you have ever seen, heard, felt or read is stored in you mind. Sometimes, we say encounter an event that the subconscious mind took as meaning that you should be overweight, and thus we have that second thought working against us.

Now, don't worry that does not mean that you are doomed to be overweight. It simply means that we now need to remove the negative thought, so that the positive suggestions may begin working.

1/2 A GALLON OF ICE CREAM

I want to be totally honest with you. I can not make you loose weight. It needs to be a cooperative endeavor.

If we go into this as kind of a partnership, where I will give it 100% and in return, you give it
100% there will be no way to fail.

I had a lady in a few years back that called me on the telephone after a weight loss session, saying it did not work.

When I asked her, what didn't it do? She replied that she left my office, and went home, and ate a half a gallon of ice cream.

When I asked her if she felt compelled to do so, or had a strong urge, she said, "No, I just wanted to see if hypnosis could stop me".

I really don't know if she thought a lighting bolt would come down and melt the ice cream, or what.

Are you ready to work as a team to get down to pounds, and stay there?

3 CATEGORIES (WEIGHT)

After this session is over you will find yourself falling into one of three categories.

About thirty percent of the people I see report that it is almost as though they never ate improperly. They never really think about over eating again.

The second category, with about another thirty percent will say, there may have been a moment when a temptation to reach for the wrong types of food entered their minds, but it faded away in just an instant. For example, some one may have brought in a plate of cookies, and automatically they started to reach for one, and then realized that they haven't done that in over a month.

The third category, with another thirty- percent may experience a little bit of a mind battle. I think I might like a piece of that cake with this cup of coffee. Yes, no, yes, no, NO I will not do it. Simply give it a few moments and the thought will fade away.

I would imagine that you could handle any one of these three categories.

CAKE

I am sure that you have heard many times how important it is to eat slowly, and chew each bite thoroughly.

There was a time in the past that I discovered the true importance of eating slowly. I was at a restaurant, and ate my meal extremely quickly. By eating quickly, I still felt hungry even though I had consumed more than enough food.

Thinking that I must still be hungry, I ordered a piece of cake for dessert.

The waitress got busy, and it took a little while for her to return with my much-needed cake. During the time that I was waiting for the cake, I started to feel full, and satisfied. I then started to

feel almost stuffed, by the time the cake arrived, and after consuming the cake I felt bloated, and miserable.

If I had eaten the meal at a slower pace, I would have given my system a chance to react and feel full, and satisfied, and thus not needing, or wanting the cake.

We tend to respond almost as much by time as we do by quantity of food. A person could cut their food intake in half, and spend twice as much time eating half the amount of food, and still be content.

HOUSE FIRE

I once had a good friend that encountered a house fire.

The fire was not to bad but the smoke damage was terrible.   It seemed as though the smoke damage went throughout the entire house.

My friend was frightened that even though the fire was out, that their little house would never be the same.

I was even amazed at the difference in their house after only one-week. The damage caused by the smoke was already fading away. There was a dramatic difference in the air.

By three weeks even that old smell of the smoke was totally gone.

By the time a month has passed by, it would have been almost impossible for anyone to even tell that there ever was smoke damage.

It is always amazing how quickly things can get back to normal, regardless of the amount of initial smoke damage. The key to success, is getting rid of the smoke, as soon possible.

CREATE DESIRE FOR

In just a moment I am going to touch your right hand. As I touch your right hand you will begin to experience a very strong urge for chocolate.

I am now touching your right hand. (TOUCH RIGHT HAND)

As you begin to feel this strong urge for chocolate, nod your head yes. (WAIT FOR RESPONSE)

Now, I would like you to create an image of yourself the way that you would like to be in the future. as you think of yourself in this way, notice how the urge for chocolate fades away.

Once the urge has faded, nod your head yes, and relax even further knowing that you are now in control of chocolates. (WAIT FOR RESPONSE)

From this moment on if you would experience an urge for chocolate, simply create an image of yourself the way that you want to be, and the urge will fade away.

NOTE TO THERAPIST: OCCASIONALLY YOUR CLIENT WILL NOT BE ABLE TO BRING BACK AN URGE FOR CHOCOLATE. IF THIS WOULD OCCUR USE THE FOLLOWING STATEMENT TO COMPLETE TNIS TECHNI QUE.

That's right now that you are hypnotized you can not bring back that old urge for chocolate. It is out of the past, and gone forever.

COMMAND

You have made a firm decision that you will never smoke again. This is your decision, and you are doing this for your own good, and your own benefit.

This means that you can and will be successful at being an ex-smoker.

You will never, ever smoke again. Not because of what I say but because it is the nature of your own mind for you to be successful.

You will never, ever again take a single puff, drag, or draw from a cigarette again.

Not because of me,, or what I have shared with you, but because you, and you alone have selected this day to be free of this unneeded smoking habit.

You are a winner.

CHANGING THE GOAL

I know that you told me that an ideal weight level for you would be 125 pounds. However would you mind if we changed the goal to 123 pounds instead?

The reason that I would like to see you change the goal, is the way that your subconscious mind reacts. I am sure that there have been many times that you have attempted to reach a goal of 125 pounds, and have failed.

So your mind has recorded failures at reaching a weight of 125 pounds. You have never tried to reach a level of 123 pounds before, so we will be starting fresh.

I realize that at a conscious level it really does not make any difference to you, whether your weight was at 123 or 125 pounds.

Our subconscious mind takes everything literally. so, striving for a goal weight that you have never tried before will eliminate the past memories of failures.

Think of it has starting fresh.

I DON'T THINK I CAN

NOTE: THE FOLLOWING STATEMENT IS A TRUISM FOR ALMOST ANY INDIVIDUAL THAT HAS NEVER BEEN HYPNOTIZED BEFORE.

I would like to share with you what most people feel about hypnosis. They do not always say it, but most people are thinking, "I believe in hypnosis on someone else, but I don't think I can be hypnotized, and even if I can, I don't know if it will help me".

So if you are sitting there with the same type, or similar thoughts, don't feel bad. More often than not people think of hypnosis with what they see on television, and if it was the way that television shows it, I wouldn't believe in it either.

First let me assure you that everyone is capable of going into hypnosis.

NOTE: FROM THIS POINT DESCRIBE THE HYPNOTIC SESSION, AND REMOVE ANY REMAINING FEARS.

HAND SHAKE

NOTE: BEGIN WITH THE CLIENT SITTING IN A COMFORTABLE CHAIR, AND PROCEED AS FOLLOWS.

T: Would you like to experience hypnosis? C: Yes I would.
After a yes response, have the client extend his or her arm to you as though you were going to be shaking hands.

TAKE THE CLIENTS HAND WITN YOUR NAND KHILE MAKING SURE TNE CLIENTS ARM IS STRAIGHT OUT IN FRONT.

I would like you to look at me for just a moment. As you focus your eyes on me; and listen to my voice, I would like you to allow things to take place

SLOWLY BEGIN RAISING, AND LOWERING THE CLIENTS ARM. THE UP AND DOWN MOVEMENT OF THE ARM SHOULD BE ABOUT THREE INCHES EACH WAY.

As I raise and lower your arm, I wonder if you have noticed yet that there is a drowsy, heavy feeling beginning to occur in and around your eyes.

Each time I raise your arm upward, that heavy feeling in those eyes can and will become stronger.

As the eyes begin to close down, it becomes increasingly more desirable to allow them to remain closed.

They are closing down all the way now. Let it happen. Want it to happen. Feel it happen now.
MAKE SPECIAL NOTE TO KHEN THE EYES BEGIN TO BLINK OR START TO CLOSE. TNIS WILL IS A SIGNAL TO THE THERAPIST TO REINFORCE THAT FEELING BY RAISING THE ARM HIGHER INTO THE AIR.

THE CLIENT WILL QUICKLY ASSOCIATE THE RAISING OF THE ARM WITH CLOSING OF THE EYES.

GOOD FEELING FOR SAYING NO

T: I would like you to recall a time in your life when you felt wonderful. A time when you felt totally in control of your own life. As you begin to recall that special wonderful time, I would like you to nod your head yes, and relax even deeper.

Good, now as I touch your right hand, I would like you now to tell me about this wonderful time.

(TOUCH RIGHT HAND)

What was happening that was so wonderful for you? C: It was a time when I graduated from high school.
T: Was that a happy time for you? C: Yes It Was.
T: Now, as I touch your right hand again, I want you to bring back those same wonderful feelings.

(TOUCH RIGHT HAND)

As you begin to feel those same wonderful feelings nod your head yes, and relax even further.

Each time I touch your right hand those wonderful feelings keep coming back stronger. (TOUCH RIGNT HAND SEVERAL TIMES)
Now, I would like you to imagine yourself being tempted to go back to the unwanted eating habits. Maybe tempted to have candy, or to over eat. Now, imagine yourself saying NO to the temptation, and notice how good you feel. (TOUCH RIGHT HAND) Now,
think of another person offering you something fattening, but you are now saying no thank you.

As you imagine yourself saying no thank you, notice how wonderful you feel. (TOUCH RIGHT HAND)

I now want you to notice that I no longer need to touch your right hand for you to experience those wonderful feelings.

Imagine yourself at home alone, and the thought of over eating comes into your mind.

Now, imagine yourself saying NO to that thought, and here comes those wonderful feelings again.

Each time you say NO to those old temptations from the past, these wonderful feelings will return even stronger.

ASKING 4 TIMES

I would like you to imagine a little boy about six or seven years old. He comes into the house, and asks his father if he could have a piece of candy. The father thinks for a moment and says no.

The boy goes back to play, but it seems like only a short time period and he is back again. May I now have a piece of candy? Once again the father says no.
Now if the child would come back a third time, he is becoming cleverer than ever before.

Dad, you're the best father in the whole world, could I now have a piece of candy? Once again the father says No

If by chance the boy would return a fourth time, now his response would be, dad never mind, forget it.

The reason that he would not ask, is that he knows what the answer would be.

Our minds work exactly in the same way. Each time you say NO to the idea of having a cigarette, the thought will fade away, soon never to bother you again.

You can now begin to enjoy saying NO, no to the idea, the thought of smoking. Something out of the past that never needs to bother you again.

YOUR FUTURE

You have decided that the time has come for you to be free of this excess weight once and for all. I want you to make sure that this is what you want. So spend a second with me now and create an image or thought of yourself in the following manner.

I want you to think of yourself with the weight of your body at or about 120 pounds. Think of yourself looking and feeling great. Dressed very nicely. Your personal life is in perfect order, your private life totally content and at ease, your job or career going well. You are in better physical shape than you have been in a number of years.

As you begin to think of yourself in this way, and this war only I would like you to nod

Conversational Hypnosis and NLP

Good, now I as going to give that wonderful image a name. Let's call this image Mary's future. Mary's future. In fact even the sound of it, is nice relaxing and fulfilling. Mary's future.

From this moment on before you would eat any type of food or drink any liquid I want you to take in a nice deep breath. As you exhale say the words to yourself, Mary's future.

As you say these powerful words to yourself, you will think of yourself in that positive way, and realize that there is no food or liquid anywhere in the world that could mean more to you than turning that image into a reality.

You will allow yourself to eat only enough to keep you alive, healthy and strong, ensuring your continuing success at reaching Mary's future.

A MANURE FIELD

You have made a decision that the time has come for you to be free of this unwanted smoking habit. I am sure that you have dozens of different, valid reasons for wanting to be a nonsmoker as of today.

In reality it has been proven that cigarette smoking does not serve any useful purpose in your daily life. In fact many people are beginning to realize a fact that growers of tobacco have known for years.

I once talked with a young man whose father owned a large tobacco farm. Even though he, and his family have been involved in growing tobacco for a number of years, he could not understand why anyone would choose to smoke.

This young man related how every year they would spread tons, and tons, of manure over the tobacco fields, and even after the tobacco was harvested the odor of the manure seemed to cling to the tobacco leaves.

This young man wanted to know why, any intelligent person would want to put an old dried up weed that has been saturated with manure in their mouth, and light it.

Although I spend my life talking, this time I was speechless.

NLP and Spirituality

STUDYING THE SEDATIVE

Spirituality for me is about finding our deepest essence as human beings, the same essence we share with every person; it connects us to everyone else. So spirit is where we become most truly ourselves, by discovering and becoming most deeply connected with others. We find ourselves in our connections with others. One metaphor occurs constantly in spiritual literature is spirituality as a journey or search, sometimes on the outside, always within.

How does NLP connect with the quest for spirit, the inner journey? I think there is some good news and some bad news about NLP in this context. Bad news first. NLP has three elements woven into its title in a rich mixture:

- Neuro- our neurology and our consciousness.
- Linguistics- our language.
- Thirdly our ability to go for outcomes: the programming part.

I would like to examine each of these three in turn. Consciousness can be a barrier if spirituality is thought of (consciously) as something to be attained, and if consciousness is assumed to be identical to self-consciousness. Consciousness is only a small part of our being, it cannot grasp the complete picture. Also something you consciously search for is different from you, the seeker. In 1934 a man named J.W. Dunne wrote an interesting book called The Serial Universe.[2] Dunne tells of a certain artist who had escaped from the lunatic asylum, where he had been confined, perhaps by mistake. This artist bought some materials: paint and easel, and set out to make a complete picture of the universe. He was not crazy enough to think he could paint the whole world, but he was determined to do the best possible job on a small section: the beautiful countryside in which he found himself. He started by painting a small picture of the surrounding countryside in the middle of his huge canvas. He drew a wonderful picture. He was extremely pleased until he noticed that something was missing. He was part of this universe and he was not in the picture. How could he add a representation of himself? The man may have been crazy but he was not mad enough to think he could paint himself standing on the ground that he had already painted as lying in front of him. So he moved his easel a little way back, asked a passing farmer to be a model and drew a

---

2   J.W. Dunne, The Serial Universe (Faber 1934)

picture of himself drawing the original picture. However, he was still not satisfied. My first picture, he thought to himself, is a picture that a man would paint who is unaware of his own existence. My second picture rectifies that. But I, the real artist am conscious and aware of my own existence, so my second picture is still incomplete. So saying, he shifted his easel.

If there could be a picture of the real world, who would be painting it?

Now language. NLP has done great work here building on the insights of Korzybski who gets credit for the famous phrase 'the map is not the territory'. The word is not the thing. As Bateson pointed out, thinking that the word is the same as the thing it describes (whatever it might be) is like going into a restaurant and eating the menu.

Chuang Tzu, the Chinese master of the fourth century AD wrote:

'The fish trap exists because of the fish. Once you have gotten the fish you can forget the trap. The rabbit snare exists because of the rabbit; once you have gotten the rabbit you can forget the snare. Words exist because of meaning. Once you have gotten the meaning you can forget the words. Where can I find a man who has forgotten words, so I can have a word with him?' [3]

Language divides the world and divides us from the world on a profound level. Language creates dualities; black or white, day or night, good and bad. Qualities are defined by their opposite. We know the good the bad and the ugly by contrasting them with the better the worse and the beautiful. So to define something like spirit using words and attributing qualities to it is paradoxically to limit it by saying it is not something else. Secondly, when we do describe something we make a distinction between us and the thing described and so immediately dissociate from it. All spiritual writings describe spirituality in metaphor. If pressed for a more direct description it is always in terms of what it is Not : 'not this, not that', (in the Upanishads) and in the Tao Te Ching: 'The Tao that can be spoken in words is not the true Tao'.

If man is basically asleep to the spiritual realm as many mystics say, then language and normal waking conscious thought are the strong and principal soporifics that not only keep him asleep, but also fool him in thinking that he is really awake. So is NLP a study of the sleeping draught?

Chuang Tzu has another story: strolling along the banks of the Hao river with his friend Hui Tzu, he says, 'See how the minnows come out and dart round as they please! That's what fish really enjoy!' Hui Tzu replies, 'You're not a fish - how do you know what fish enjoy?' Chuang Tzu has a retort however, 'You're not I, so how do you know I don't know what fish enjoy?'

Hui Tzu comes back again, 'I'm not you, so I certainly don't know what you know. On the other hand you're certainly not a fish - so that still proves you don't know what fish enjoy!'

Chuang Tzu has the last word, 'Let's go back to the original question please. You asked me how I know what fish enjoy- so you already knew I knew it when you asked the question. I know it by standing here beside the Hao.'

Now the programming part of NLP - the ways we act with purpose to achieve outcomes. Outcomes are a very important part of NLP, they are the starting point for any NLP intervention. A basic NLP presupposition is that everything we do has a purpose. Conscious minds set outcomes. We set them and make sure they are expressed in the positive, are specified appropriately, within our influence, and appropriately sized. We make sure we have an evidence procedure for knowing when we have arrived, and attempt to make them ecological, although how our unaided conscious mind is supposed to do this, is hard to know. If outcomes are ends, things to be attained, the 'how to', the means are not specified, and yet how we go about achieving the outcome will affect what we get and the consequences. It's the 'how' that counts.

The books of the American Anthropologist Carlos Casteneda, are unacknowledged influences on NLP. Casteneda writes in his book Journey to Ixtlan[4], or rather reports his mentor Don Juan, talking about the spirit of the warrior. The warrior is impeccable. The warrior sets outcomes knowing full well they may be totally trivial, but commits to them totally as if they were to be his or her last act on earth. The warrior is totally aligned and totally him or herself, so the resulting action has a purity and a focus that does not come from the outcome, but from the process of acting. It's interesting that the root of the word impeccable means 'unable to sin'.

Casteneda is asking us to act 'As If' the quality of what we do is the most important thing in the world - regardless of what we are trying to achieve. As our lives are so complex and systemically intertwined the idea of outcomes as isolated occurrences are an illusion anyway. The quality of the journey is the important thing. Outcomes 'come out' of how we act to achieve what we want.

The road to Hell is paved with good intentions. This usually means wonderful outcomes and appalling means. The greater, the more refined and spiritual the outcome the more mayhem and havoc can be wreaked in trying to achieve it, once you accept that the end justifies the means. With an end outcome defined for the good of all, people have felt totally justified in committing atrocities trying to achieve it.

There is a character called Shigalov in Dostoevsky's novel The Possessed.[5] Shigalov has founded a Utopian system that will redeem present society. He warns his co-conspirators that even the shortest explanation of his system will take ten evening sessions to explain. And the system is not yet complete. He goes on: 'I am perplexed by my own data, and my conclusion is in direct contradiction to the original idea from which I started. Starting from unlimited freedom, I arrived at unlimited tyranny. I will add, however, that there is no other solution of the social formula than mine.' Here his friends started to laugh at him, which was probably the most sensible thing they could have done.

---

4   Carlos Casteneda, Journey to Ixtlan (Simon and Schuster 1972)
5   Fyodor Dostoevsky, The Possessed (various editions)

It is possible to argue the only humane definition of peace is actually a negative one: the absence of violence, because every positive definition will lead to violence in trying to attain it. This does not fit well with NLP well-formedness outcome conditions. Although good intentions pave the road to Hell, one of the important contributions of NLP is to separate behaviour from intention. So while marching towards the underworld we can at least acknowledge that this is not exactly where we want to go. In fact we want to go in the opposite direction, only the signposts got a little confused. By explicitly recognising the intention behind the behaviour we have a choice of moving logical levels. There is another NLP presupposition: everyone makes the best choice they can given their model of the world, but this does not excuse or explain that some terrible things are done in the world, NLP has to recognise this. Recognition, does not mean justification. Intentions are positive in the sense of being directed at some outcome as opposed to positive as being 'good' in some way. I do see a interesting clash between the focus on outcomes from NLP and spirituality as the quality of the journey. Perhaps setting process outcomes is one answer. End outcomes are what you get at the end, (eg. in sport winning the race), process outcomes are about how you are going to act in order to achieve it. Perhaps NLP could address the issue of well formedness conditions for process outcomes. How could you begin to think about setting an outcome to act impeccably?

That's the bad news. The good news is that precisely because NLP concerns itself so closely with linguistics, outcomes and consciousness, we have a fine way of exploring these issues. In another age old metaphor, if you perceive yourself in a prison, a good place to start your escape plan is to study the walls, bars, and habits of the guards in detail. Only by knowing intimately what constrains you can you hope to escape it. NLP studies maps with the insistence that they are to be separated from the territory they represent. NLP's contribution to spirituality can be to carefully map the areas in its title. Spirituality itself will always begin just beyond the edge of the map. I believe Spirituality is territorial. NLP also insists on sensory based descriptions and the importance of sensory experience. This is congruent with spirituality which is about experience. Mystics through out the ages tell the same metaphors about spiritual experience, regardless of historical period, or the organised belief systems they subscribe to. They insist on the importance of the experience. Words fall short of the experience like stones thrown at the stars. We throw a lot of stones, some may be well aimed, but they still bring us no closer, nor do they help you appreciate their beauty.

A final story from Chuang Tzu, talking to his friend Hui Tzu. Hui Tzu said to Chuang Tzu, 'Your words are useless!'
Chuang Tzu said, 'A man has to understand the useless before you can talk to him about the useful. The earth is certainly vast and broad, though a man uses no more of it than the area he puts his feet on. If however, you were to dig away all the earth from around his feet until you reached the Yellow Springs (The Underworld) then would the man still be able to make use of it?'
'No, it would be useless,' said Hui Tzu.
'It is obvious then,' said Chuang Tzu, 'that the useless has its uses.'

www.ingramcontent.com/pod-product-compliance
Lightning Source LLC
Chambersburg PA
CBHW081226040426
42445CB00016B/1905